CORRECTION OFFICER!

The Other Side Of The Wall**

Joe Calitri

CONTENTS

Return To Daylight

Life In The Lockup

Banishment

A Brief Flirtation With Promotion

Transportation

Attention Deficit

The "Uncivil" War

The Disciplinary Office

Adversarial Administrations

Employee Relations

The Assignment Office

Retaliation

Casualties

Cast Of Characters

Correction Officer's Prayer

Epilogue

Prologue

June 28, 1996, was my final work day on the other side of the wall. Like so many 7-3 shifts before, I was assigned to the segregation unit, called the RB, along with several other experienced and capable officers. After completing my various routine duties, I received permission from the lieutenant in charge to spend my last hour canvassing the institution to say farewell to many good friends and co-workers with whom I had developed such a fine camaraderie over the years.

While crossing the Administration Building on my way into the prison yard, I paused to consider the surrealism of the moment. Retirement papers were in order; I would be utilizing my final five weeks of earned vacation time for the entire month of July; I made use of all of my accrued sick leave, selling back a measly 20 hours for 20 cents on the dollar; and my last official day on the payroll was to be August 3rd.

Oh, what a rush!

Every event; every item of interest; every opinion, point of view and analysis in this book is written from memory. My short-term recollection suffers the natural effects of the aging process, but fortunately I have been blessed with a very accurate long-term remembrance. My Correction Officer career began more than four decades ago and ended after twenty years, but a great many experiences still easily come to mind. My occasional bizarre dreams about those days are quite vivid!

Introduction

The history of human incarceration can be traced back to the beginning of civilized social order. It is common knowledge that people have been confined in jails and prisons for a plethora of reasons; from violations of criminal and civil laws to being victims of political unrest and prisoners of war. Lord knows that there have been too many persons wrongfully accused and imprisoned due to the imperfection of humanity and criminal justice systems, but for the most part convicted felons, at least in the United States, are dealt with fairly and honestly. The loss of one's personal freedom is widely considered to be proper punishment for criminal behavior. Many folks disagree, though, and demand a more biblical style of justice. I happen to side with the latter.

Those of us who served and continue serving to protect the public by keeping convicted felons confined within jails and correctional facilities are identified by a number of titles. Throughout my career, we called ourselves **Correction**

Officers. For the sake of consistency, I will refer to these two words and capitalize them for emphasis. The adjectives "correctional" and "corrections" are sometimes used and are equally acceptable. Sheriff's deputies maintain county jails, and female prison officers are sometimes called matrons. For decades, if not centuries, Correction Officers were called "prison guards," obviously because their responsibilities were to guard inmates and make sure they stayed imprisoned. However, modern day Correction Officers take great offense being referred to as "guards," with good reason. This profession has grown into a complex system of care, custody and control, and involves much more than just standing around eyeballing convicts.

Anyone expecting to find nonstop action, adventure and violence in my story will be a bit disappointed. That's not to say that such events never happened, just that life in a medium security prison like the Massachusetts Correctional Institution at Norfolk scarcely resembles old prison movies about hell holes like Devil's Island, Alcatraz or Attica. Neither is it this way in most, if not all, modern day prisons. My career as a Correction Officer was similar to that of other public safety professionals like police officers and firefighters; there were frequent moments of inactivity amidst the routines of the day, but when "the shit hit the fan," that's when we earned our pay.

We officers were trained in various degrees of disturbance control, fire response, CPR, and emergency first aid, but a successful shift was one in which we never had to utilize such skills. Police officers are provided with an array of equipment, such as firearms, vehicles and self-defense tools to help them effectively perform their duties. Firefighters wear protective clothing and have an assortment of devices and machines at their disposal. New Correction Officers at MCI Norfolk in 1976 were issued only an aluminum two-cell flashlight and a whistle. Over time, a few two-way radios were made available to supervisory staff and some yard officers, but a considerable amount of communication was conducted through an institutional loudspeaker system. Handcuffs and restraint equipment were confined to the outer control area and were only available by request, even in the segregation unit. *That* was hard to fathom! Only after one officer was assaulted and seriously injured by an inmate while escorting him to be locked up were officers assigned to Quad duty allowed to carry handcuffs. Several years passed before officers were regularly provided with cuffs, radios, or body alarms. An arsenal of restraints was finally kept permanently on all three floors of the segregation unit, and riot control and extraction team equipment was made easily accessible in the Administration Building.

One of my father's friends asked him if he was worried about me working in such an environment. Dad claimed he was not, since he believed I had "the old equalizer" on me, referring to a firearm. When I explained to them that we carried no weapons of any kind while working inside the walls, their silence was deafening. A Correction Officer's profession is not called "the toughest beat" for nothing!

An Unexpected Career

The summer of 1974 was a strange and confusing time for me. I had finished as much college education as I could tolerate and was trying to shake off the effects of an overwhelming wave of apathy which left me unsure of future aspirations. My beloved father had been pushing me through private high school and beyond with the insistence that I pursue a medical career, as he did, or one in a similar field of science. My grades in this curriculum were good, but my forte, and my passion, were written and oral composition. I was locked in quite a conundrum.

Age-wise, my father and mother were two generations older than I, having adopted me in 1952 when I was six days old. They grew up in a time when parents too often forced their children into particular career directions rather than giving them the opportunity to make their own choices. Coming from an old-fashioned Italian family, when Dad spoke, my sister and I listened; when Dad told us to do something, we did it.

My father insisted that I wasn't getting an adequate education in the West Bridgewater public school system, so he forced me to take the entrance exam and then enrolled me in the private Thayer Academy in Braintree, Massachusetts. After graduation, I was accepted to attend Hartwick College in Oneonta, New York. Without the advice of a counselor, Dad more or less created my first semester course itinerary by selecting Biology, Chemistry and Calculus, claiming that anything that wasn't math or science was essentially "cooking and sewing" and a waste of time. He had my best interests at heart but knew nothing of college requirements in 1969. His frame of reference came from 1929.

Sadly, I disappointed dear old Dad by not following in his footsteps, but the medical field was not my calling. I told him that if I couldn't do that job the way he did; and I knew I couldn't; then I shouldn't continue to waste my time and his money. I left Hartwick after one year and finished my education at Eastern Nazarene College in Quincy, Massachusetts. My journalism professor there asked if I would like a job writing for the school newspaper and I jumped at the opportunity, but his effort to obtain this for me was unsuccessful. He then asked if I would like a position with the Quincy Patriot Ledger newspaper. I was excited about the possibility, told him I'd welcome such a job, but the teacher

failed to come through again; two disappointments in a row.

My search then began for employment in the world of Marine Biology, after earning perfect grades in that science. I was a certified scuba diver and had received a behind-the-scenes introduction to the New England Aquarium in Boston while I was in college. When I applied for a job at that facility, however, I was told they were only accepting volunteers and had no paid positions available. I also visited the Woods Hole Oceanographic Institute, but the best that organization could offer me was mowing lawns and cleaning fish. A promised job as a diver at the Nantasket Beach Aquarium fell through when the installation abruptly closed. The Cape Cod Aquarium in Yarmouth advertised for someone to assist in training sea lions, but the application line was hundreds of people long, and I had no desire to wait all day for one long-shot position. I even went so far as to apply for a spot on Jacques Cousteau's research ship, Calypso, along with several thousand other candidates, but was not chosen.

While catching my breath from all the employment misadventures, I provided maintenance and landscaping service for my parents, dabbling in other odd jobs along the way. I had no idea, however, that my father had been investigating employment at the Bridgewater, Massachusetts, prison complex on my behalf. He used his influence with the local police chief who contacted one of the deputy superintendents at Bridgewater, and then Dad asked me if I would be interested in such a position. I gave it some consideration, was not overly enthused, but met with the deputy to learn about the opportunity. He told me that I couldn't be hired directly at that time, recommending that I take the Correction Officer Civil Service examination and wait to be called.

Incredibly coincidently, I was mowing the lawn around my father's office one morning when I noticed a familiar patient walking in. "Charlie" was a few years older than I, a very personable guy. He wore a large bandage on his head and when I inquired as to what happened to him, he replied, "Oh, no big deal, I got 'piped' up at Walpole!" He was a Correction Officer at the maximum security Massachusetts Correctional Institution at Walpole, now called Cedar Junction. I began second-guessing the idea of applying for such a job while listening to this wounded little guy tell me how officers were frequently being assaulted there.

My father talked to "Charlie" about my becoming a Correction Officer and "Charlie" also advised me to take the Civil Service test for that occupation. Being more or less desperate for a job, I applied for the exam and passed it in 1975,

but it would be almost a year before I was called into service.

During the process of taking the written corrections test, receiving a brief medical exam and an unremarkable interview, I had expressed a desire to work at MCI Bridgewater because it was close to my home. I was required to select two more preferences of institutions to be assigned in the event there were no positions for me in Bridgewater. Knowing very little about the system at that time, I added MCI Norfolk and the women's facility, MCI Framingham. After seeing my friend "Charlie" with a head wound and listening to his tales of MCI Walpole, I wanted no part of that nuthouse. Nor did I have any desire to work in the zombie world of Bridgewater State Hospital for the Criminally Insane, but I was willing to gamble on one of the other facilities within that complex. In May of

1976 I received orders to report to Norfolk and on the 31st of that month I began my Correction Officer career.

The Norfolk Way

[As you digest the pages of my Correction Officer adventure, bear in mind that I retired from the system in 1996 and significant changes to the structure and

operation of MCI Norfolk have likely been made since then. Warning: Harsh Language Ahead]

MCI Norfolk was originally founded in 1927 as the Norfolk Prison Colony. It was conceived by sociologist and penologist Howard B. Gill, who was appointed as its first superintendent in 1931. Gill was replaced in 1934 by Deputy Superintendent Maurice N. Winslow after an escape by four inmates, and in the mid-1950s the facility was renamed the Massachusetts Correctional Institution at Norfolk. MCI Norfolk is the largest state prison in Massachusetts, housing criminally sentenced males. It is classified as medium security because of its maximum confinement wall contrasting a minimum interior, has an average daily population of around 1,500 inmates, and can house almost 100 in a separate segregation unit. The count was only about 500 inmates when I started in 1976.

In its past prison colony design, Norfolk engaged in agriculture using inmate labor, including crop raising and a functioning piggery. Even though the state's prison system once offset certain costs by utilizing facility resources, the practice was phased out over the years. At the time I started in 1976, the only remaining symbol of the agricultural way was the donation of barrels of prison food waste to a local pig farmer.

A small community of several homes, called "The Oval," was constructed near the southern wall of the prison. A number of officers and their families lived there and were charged minimal rent in exchange for being readily available to respond to prison emergencies. By the time the 1980s rolled around, a couple of the buildings were being used for training classrooms and the rest were closed down.

The physical structure of the institution is unique, to say the least. Unlike familiar photographs and documentaries of prisons like Sing Sing and San Quentin, and old movies of riotous cell blocks, the Norfolk I first knew was essentially a college campus surrounded by four approximately thirty-foot-high concrete walls, each roughly a quarter-mile long, topped with electrified barbed wire and five observation towers.

An interior chain-link and razor-wire fence created a "dead zone" perhaps ten yards wide between it and the wall. Supposedly, any inmate attempting to escape was at risk of being shot if discovered inside that zone, but I am unaware of that theory ever being tested. Number One Tower, positioned at the southwest corner of the walls, controls the electric doors of the Vehicle Trap, where delivery and service trucks are inspected before entering and leaving the prison. Towers numbered Two, Three and Four are stationed at the other wall corners. Number Five Tower sits on the north wall between Two and Three Towers and oversees the Pedestrian Trap and Administration Building walkway, operating ingress and egress doors for staff and visitors. The officers in One and Five Towers can confine vehicles and people respectively, if necessary, by securing the doors on each end of their holding areas.

The Pedestrian Trap corridor stretches from the Gatehouse control room to the first Five Tower door. The upper floors of the building provide a recreation/roll call room, plus several bedrooms and bunk house arrangements for employees who choose to sleep on site. In the basement are a staff exercise area, handball court, and indoor firearms range.

Officers inside the control room of the Gatehouse maintain vigilance of the prison's operation from a secure command area. Once these officers authorize people to enter the prison, pedestrians are required to pass through a metal detector and their belongings are searched for contraband material. A locked room on the left side of the corridor is used for searching suspicious visitors and another on the right serves to process and prepare inmates for travel in and out of the facility. The officer manning Five Tower then manually opens one large steel door for people to enter the trap, closes that door, and opens the other leading onto the path towards the Administration Building; never are both doors to be opened simultaneously. Towards the end of my career, the Five Tower doors were electrically motorized, able to be opened by the press of a button instead of pushing and pulling large, metal handles.

The Ad Building, as it was called, contains offices for the superintendent, deputy superintendents and administrative personnel. During my years of service, the second floor was home to the Personnel Office, C.O. Assignment Office, inmate photo ID area and some conference rooms, while the Treasurer's Office and other support staff were on the third floor.

Steel-barred gates and metal doors separate the Hospital Unit and Receiving Building (RB) on either end of the Ad Building, and until the mid-1980s, another barred gate stood at the entry to an attached Visiting Room. A new, stand-alone visitor's area was eventually constructed. A fourth gate allows entrance into the prison yard, as does a fifth gate that is rarely used. One or two officers are assigned to operate the aptly named "Ad Gate" position. The first holds keys to each barred door and manually opens and closes them. The second officer's post is outside the gate leading into the yard where he pat searches inmates before they enter the Ad Building. Other officers in the old visiting room waiting area process inmates for escorted trips to court, outside hospitals or transfers.

Walking the pathway into the prison yard, the first building encountered is the Community Services Department (CSD). It's designed with a central auditorium where inmates can watch movies or other entertainment, a meeting room on one end and a chapel on the other, with several smaller offices in the basement. Further inside the prison are eighteen "resident" housing units, built in blocks of three, numbered One, Two and Six Blocks on the east side, and Three, Four and Seven Blocks on the west. I never knew why there was no Five Block but when I retired in 1996, a prefabricated Eight Block was under construction in the West Field. In the center of the institution is a large rectangular walkway with a grassy interior called "The Quad," and officers assigned to patrol that area are responsible for maintaining security and keeping convicts from loitering there. At the south edge of the Quad hangs a large, black, horseshoe-shaped steel girder called "the gong;" the prison's most notable icon. An inmate would strike the gong with a sledge hammer a number of times signaling the other inmates to return to their units for major counts prior to daily mealtimes, and then announcing when the count was clear so they could move about again.

The East and West Fields contain softball diamonds and jogging paths which can be monitored by officers on the ground and in the towers. An outdoor basketball court sits at the rear of Six Block, and at the end of the East Field a modern athletic center was constructed, containing indoor basketball courts, weight rooms, handball courts, and billiard area....courtesy of the once "proud liberal" Massachusetts governor, Michael Dukakis. This building has been described as one that was "every bit as good as the University of Oklahoma fieldhouse." Millions of taxpayer dollars were allocated by the leftist Massachusetts government to give convicted felons more accommodations than many law-abiding citizens will ever have. Nice, huh?

At the rear of the prison, collectively called the "South Yard," there was a greenhouse, an abandoned brick power plant, the Maintenance building, Mainline Kitchen, an inmate laundry, Vocational Education center, and the Industries building during my time in service. The administration also transformed an old indoor gym and boxing ring into the South Yard Housing Unit as bed space for a number of older inmates. Near Four Tower at the junction of the south and east walls rests an old concrete blockhouse, popularly known as "Hollywood." It was once used as Norfolk's version of "the hole," as seen in numerous prison movies. If I remember correctly, there were eight caged cells inside that were used as disciplinary punishment for problematic inmates. Those who endured the confinement were then considered "celebrities" for being sent there, hence the building's nickname. It had long ceased being utilized when I arrived in 1976 and served simply as a storage area.

Aerial Photo of MCI Norfolk

A network of tunnels lined with steam pipes and electric wiring runs beneath the complex, through which inmates push food carts from the Mainline Kitchen to dumbwaiters beneath the individual housing units. Inmate housemen pull the food up by hand and prepare it for serving.

Training

As of this writing, there is a ten-week Basic Training Academy program conducted at the Shirley Correctional Complex where recruits become familiar with Department of Correction policies, procedures and equipment, while working on personal physical conditioning. I would imagine that this training is modernized and state-of-the-art.

On Monday, May 31, 1976, I was joined by three other new officers. We were met by the MCI Norfolk training supervisor, "Vito," in the Gatehouse lobby, and off we trekked for one entire week; actually, only five days of "OJT;" on-the-job training. There was no Academy available then. It was closed indefinitely for budgetary reasons, so I was told. The Department of Correction was hiring individual officers "off the street."

The first hours of Day One were spent on an uneventful guided tour of the prison with very informal explanations and descriptions of the operation. We saw inmates walking about in an open interior yard, looked at the concrete walls and observation towers from both sides, then visited the inside of Five Tower, located in the middle of the north wall. The officer assigned there controlled the prison's entrance and exit doors, being able to look down through an opening into the area between them designed as a securable "trap" to help prevent escapes. He viewed the walkway into the Administration Building plus the Pedestrian Trap corridor leading from the tower to the Gatehouse control room.

We scrutinized the weapons within the tower; a .38 caliber revolver which the officer was to keep on his person, and a locked glass case containing a 12-gauge shotgun, M-1 Carbine rifle, and a vintage Thompson submachine gun. I was a bit intimidated but not deterred. One point of interest was a specialized patch covering what appeared to be a hole in one of the tower windows. The training supervisor said, "That's where some asshole fired a bullet through the window and into the Ad Building door. Don't you guys ever do that!" I didn't think we needed to be told, but we got the message. As a side note, the officer who accidentally fired a .38 round through that window became a good friend. We worked on the 4-12 shift, were scuba diving partners, and competed together on the institution pistol team. He never described the tower incident to me, simply saying that no one would ever know what really happened.

When we broke for lunch, I sat and talked with fellow rookies "Frank," a nervous young man who was also studying law in college, and "Rhino," a short, stocky 19-year-old weight lifter. The only memory I have of the fourth member of our group is that he excused himself to go to his car and never returned. It's true that a Correction Officer's job is not for everyone, but this guy apparently didn't even want to give it a chance.

While the Department of Correction attempted to portray itself as a paramilitary-type organization, it bore no resemblance to either the United States armed forces or any law enforcement organization. The chain of command identifications had more in common with a business operation. The superintendent was ultimately in charge of MCI Norfolk, but in June of 1976 there was no one officially in that position. The Deputy Superintendent of Security ran the institution as an acting superintendent until one was formally appointed. There was also a Deputy Superintendent of Classification, who oversaw inmate placements, and a number of Assistant Deputy Superintendents (ADS) who commanded the three shifts of officers. The position of Director of Security was created later. Supervisor Correction Officers monitored general operations and filled in as shift commanders when needed. Senior Correction Officers presided over specific areas of the prison and worked directly with the line officers. Even our uniforms gave a less-than-authoritative appearance, making us look like bus drivers or private security guards. We wore khaki shirts, pants and hard-brimmed hats in the warm weather, and dark green pants, blazers, overcoats, hats, and black ties during the colder months. All I could picture was the way officers dressed in old prison movies.

Our next stop on Supervisor "Vito's" tour was the maximum security section, referred to as the Receiving Building (RB). The intent of the RB was to provide housing for new convicts while they were being processed for transfer into the general population. The first two floors of this unit were called the Reception Diagnostic Center (RDC), operated by a separate but distinct group of officers. The RDC name sounded more like an area of a hospital, but the liberal ideology of the day controlled the sugar-coating of harsh-sounding language to give prisons a kinder, gentler image.

The third floor of the RB held thirty-nine individual cells closed by solid steel doors with food slots and observation windows, used to isolate inmates with disciplinary or protective custody issues. The bottom two floors had slightly fewer numbers of cells, but the doors were identical. "Frank," "Rhino" and I met the senior in charge inside the secured control post, along with another officer in civilian clothes who had started a week or so before we did but had yet to receive his uniform. Suddenly, the deafening sound of pounding on metal doors joined with that of smashing porcelain and shouting of inmates from the various cells. What the hell did I get myself into?

Supervisor "Vito" told us trainees to go down the tier and support the veteran officers who had responded to the disturbance, saying, "Surround that cell." Surround a cell? How do we do *that?* When we looked at him with skepticism he added, "You're officers, too!" I guessed it didn't matter that we had no experience or training. We followed the order and I received my first introduction to the phrase "shit hitting the fan;" on Day One, no less! There were two black inmates, brothers "Harry" and "Warren," who were obviously upset about something and had smashed the porcelain toilets and sinks in their cells in an effort to create a flood. In the process, "Harry" had cut both of his hands and was bleeding profusely. The prison doctor and male nurse "Jim" arrived to bandage "Harry's" injuries, two uniformed officers handcuffed the prisoner and escorted him to the facility's hospital. "Warren" then needed to be removed from his cell, and what I witnessed was nothing compared to the formal extraction procedures I engaged in years later. One tall, husky officer named "Mike," wearing only a helmet and faceguard for his protection, pulled the inmate from his cell, held a wooden baton to his throat from behind and said, "If you move, I'll break your neck." "Warren" walked obediently with his hands up and was transferred out of the unit.

Incredibly, he was not wearing any restraints. Come to find out, there were no handcuffs, waist chains, or leg irons on hand in the RB, and the cuffs placed on "Harry" had to be brought in from the Gatehouse. There was definitely something wrong with that picture.

At shift's end, I began putting the events of the day into context and thought, "What an introduction to this job; a 'rip-out' during my first experience on the other side of the wall!"

But, I figured after taking the Civil Service exam and waiting almost a year to be hired, I wasn't about to throw the opportunity away. Our next couple of training days amounted to being introduced to a few administrators, then being split up and assigned to shadow veteran yard officers during their rounds. It was difficult trying to absorb all the small details but was not an uncomfortable feeling.

Later in the week, we three rookies were escorted to an outdoor firing range by the armorer, "Don," who was also the Gatehouse Senior on the 12am to 8am shift, and familiarized with the weapons we had seen in Five Tower. I had no proficiency with firearms at that time but handled them well. Shooting targets with the .38 caliber Smith and Wesson revolver came easily for "Rhino" and me, but "Frank" was having difficulty. He was hitting logs and rocks with no problem, but his assigned target was undamaged. We took turns with the old World War II M-1 Carbine and again, "Rhino" and I showed confidence. Poor "Frank" couldn't grasp the instructions and kept ejecting live rounds after each shot rather than just pulling the trigger semi-automatically. The 12-gauge shotgun and Thompson submachine gun were intimidating but not difficult for two of us to fire. "Frank," on the other hand, had to return another day for additional training.

CSD, Quad, Housing Units Overview

Donning The Uniform

On the last day of training, we received our khaki uniforms, flashlights, whistles, and assignments. There were two openings on the 4pm to 12am shift and one for the 12am to 8am. "Frank" requested the Midnight Shift, which was fine with "Rhino" and me, and we were told to begin on Sunday, June 6, our official starting date. We earned no seniority during training. I remember precisely that our starting gross salary was $196.70 a week. Sadly, a short time into his career, "Frank" was assaulted and injured by an inmate, and I learned that he resigned not long afterwards.

At MCI Norfolk, the three standard shifts contain a number of set days off, called bids, arranged by the administration. When officers changed shifts, transferred, retired, or left the department, their positions were vacated and could be posted for other officers to request via bid slips, awarded by seniority. It's fair to say that the 8-4 shift with Saturdays and Sundays off was the most desirable. A handful of officers were part of a special 10pm to 6am group, each of whom joined with two members of the 4-12 and then two from the 12-8 to count inmates in the housing units each hour of that shift. Officers on Sick Relief and Vacation Relief shifts would fill in for others on leave. In 1976, there were eighteen inmate housing units resembling dormitories, each staffed by a plain-clothed officer on 6am to 2pm and 2pm to 10pm shifts, except units 3-2 and 6-3 which were empty and under repair at the time. House Officer positions were the only specific time-off and placement-assignments allowed to be requested. Other bids were for shifts and days off only. Management seemed to believe that officers in civilian clothes controlling the units would be less intimidating to the poor, sensitive convicts, but years later, House Officers were placed in uniforms. I guess the inmates weren't very intimidated by an officer's wardrobe one way or another.

There were also three statuses of officers at the time; permanent, temporary and provisional; the first two based upon Civil Service exam scores and the dates that the agency chose to certify them. The few that were hired provisionally had yet to take the test. One aspect of the bid system allowed officers to actually retain a permanent position on one shift as a fall back, while working a temporary slot on another shift. Officers could be "bumped" from their

preferable temporary bids back to less desirable permanent bids in a rare domino effect of position realignments.

There's no need to create headaches among readers by trying to explain the intricacies. Just bear with me.

The Civil Service test I took in 1975 had an assortment of curious questions like, "Do you prefer roses or daffodils, violins or machine guns?" Stunningly, I received the lowest passing grade, 70, and was the last officer made permanent from that particular list. I inquired as to how a college-educated man could score at the bottom of the class while some characters, who had difficulty figuring out where to print their names, scored higher. I was told that the test was a "psychological evaluation" to determine "thought patterns" in prospective officers and look for "consistency." Gee, that was comforting. So much for giving honest answers. The Civil Service tests that were given years later had apparently changed format, showing clocks and asking times of day, among other questions, and requiring scores of 100 or high 90s for applicants to be made permanent. Fortunately for me, my long wait for permanency was uneventful and passed quickly.

During the 4-12 (later 3-11) shift, events of the day came to a close and officers were assigned specific tasks, such as securing the Mainline Kitchen, driving inmates to collect food waste, monitoring activities in the CSD, the OPD medication line, and observing inmates in the East and West Fields. We conducted inmate counts at 10pm and 11pm, then turned over that responsibility to the 12-8 (later 11-7) shift.

"Rhino" and I were the two newest temporaries on the 4-12. He was assigned Wednesdays and Thursdays off, I was given Thursdays and Fridays, but I caught some flak from a few of the temporary officers who were senior to me for having Fridays off, even though it was the shift commander's decision. The controversy faded quickly as the bid system maintained its fluidity and I eventually won a posted bid for Wednesdays and Thursdays off. Then came the learning process.

Some officers, including females called matrons at the time, were assigned to operate the Gatehouse outer control where they processed staff and visitors through a metal detector and coordinated much of the shift operations. One officer manned each of five security towers mounted on the exterior walls, while others handled posts such as the Administration Building gate, the RB and the Hospital. My first duty was inside the yard where I was paired with an officer who had started only three months earlier. That was easily enough time for one to become familiar with the particular responsibilities of the assignment.

There were five other pairs of officers as well, and we were designated by the units whose inmates we were expected to count at 10pm and 11pm before end of shift. There were also specific duties connected with these assignments. My partner and I were in "The Deuces," the Two Block, where we were required to maintain security in the Mainline Kitchen, and then count units 2-1, 2-2 and 2-3 later on. It was an interesting first official day in uniform.

For the sake of clarity, the officers counting the One Block had to monitor the inmate Outpatient medication line and parts of the East Field, then count units 1-1, 1-2 and 1-3. Three

Block supervised the Community Service Department building (CSD), watched the West Field and counted units 3-1, 4-1, 4-2 and 4-3. Those in the Six Block patrolled "the Quad" and counted 6-1, 6-2 and 7-3. One of the Seven Block officers monitored activity in the various rooms of the inner control school building, also called the Officer In Charge (OIC). The second drove inmates in a utility vehicle as they picked up food waste from the blocks, and then both counted units 3-3, 7-1, and 7-2.

Camaraderie On The 4-12

I learned early on that MCI Norfolk had been the scene of two devastating firearm assaults by inmates prior to my start date. In 1973, a woman smuggled two handguns into the institution and gave them to the inmate she was visiting. He proceeded to shoot and kill an officer and an Industries Instructor before shooting his accomplice and taking his own life. There was no metal detector in use at the time with which to uncover weapons before they were brought into the institution. In 1975, another convicted felon somehow obtained a handgun and seriously injured two officers before being wounded and captured. These events were chilling reminders of the dangers associated with this profession and served to heighten my awareness of the surroundings.

A surprising reality of the inner workings of the prison in 1976 was that certain groups of inmates helped maintain relative order. The Two Block units were given interesting nicknames; 2-1 was called "Little Italy," 2-2 was "Little Harlem," and 2-3 was named "Little San Juan." These buildings housed Italian organized crime members, black criminals and Puerto Rican inmates respectively. Though some theories suggest that forced integration serves a purpose, such was not the case at MCI Norfolk. So-called "Mafia underboss Enrico," serving a life sentence for murder, was allowed to have two rooms inside unit 2-1; one to sleep in and another for storing his property. Other inmates had single rooms. He lived close to the Hospital Outpatient entrance where he obtained his daily medication, and was chaperoned everywhere he went by strategically placed underlings. Some of these inmates actually tended to vegetable garden plots in the West Field, and one former mob executioner planted and cultivated flowers on both sides of the walkway between Five Tower and the Ad Building.

Norfolk's inmates were allowed to elect two "camp co-chairmen" as liaisons between the population and the administration. In some respects, the prison ran itself because these inmates, with the support of many high-profile crime figures, maintained a degree of order. They were more concerned about completing or shortening their sentences than causing trouble. More than one convict required medical attention after disrespecting a member of the "Italian-American club."

As the years passed, older inmates were paroled, released, or died in prison, and a new generation of younger, more aggressive and problematic inmates began

overpopulating the institution.

On day two of my new shift I was looking forward to meeting my girlfriend after work, but 4-12 Supervisor "Chris" came into the unit where my partner and I were waiting to leave and told me that I was "drafted." What the hell did *that* mean? I hadn't heard that word since 1969 when I was watching the Viet Nam War Selective Service lottery on television. "Chris" explained to me that the Midnight Shift was shorthanded and since there were no volunteers from the   4-12 to work overtime, the shift commander instituted a reverse seniority draft which forced me to stay on duty for another eight hours. Good friggin' grief! "Chris" was also working overtime. He brought me a free meal, and I was allowed a telephone call to cancel my date. At least I was getting my mandatory draft out of the way, would drop to the bottom of the next list and not be forced again any time soon. I remained in the Three

Block to continue conducting inmate counts with two 12-8 officers, "Brev" and "Brad," but after making our introductions and completing the first hourly round, these two men proceeded to fall asleep inside our base unit, expecting *me* to remain awake and to alert them for the next count or if a supervisor was coming to check on us. To say I was stunned would be an understatement. Here I was, tired from my first eight hours, now working a double shift, and these supposedly fresh officers nodded off after less than an hour on duty? I didn't dare fall asleep for fear of being disciplined or fired if caught, so that was one long night, and not an overly enjoyable first experience with the Midnight Shift!

The next unexpected surprise came on Monday of my third week on the 4-12 shift. The employee information paperwork I signed upon being hired contained a union membership card. The options were to join the organization and receive full representation or pay an agency service fee solely for contractual benefits. I was never a fan of "big umbrella" unions but I figured I might as well obtain as much as possible for my dues. As I drove into the parking lot, I was surrounded by a group of officers who stopped me and asked if I was going to work. Obviously that was why I arrived, but they told me that our union, the American Federation of State, County and Municipal Employees (AFSCME) had ordered a work stoppage over contractual wage issues. Then I noticed the picket signs. Here I was, brand new on the job and now I had to strike?

My first thought was the fear of being fired, since I was only a temporary employee. I hurriedly searched out the local union president, Officer "Everett," and he assured me that no one was going to be terminated because of the situation. He told me to continue reporting to the prison for my normal shifts and join the picket lines for the duration of the strike. Shortly after being given this information, our angry shift commander, ADS "Arnold," announced that all days off and vacations were canceled. I wondered how much worse this situation was going to get.

There were two choices given to union members during the strike; join the picket line or cross it and report for work. The first would keep me in good standing with my fellow officers but I would not receive any salary; the second would keep the paychecks coming but I'd be working multiple duties, long hours and be considered a pariah by the rank and file. I chose to remain on the picket line and ride out the storm. I stayed with my fellow officers on Tuesday and Wednesday of that week while contract negotiations continued. A couple of strikers attempted to prevent service vehicles from entering the institution, but State Police officers were monitoring the activity and ordered that no vehicles be impeded. We still expected to receive paychecks from the previous week and on the front steps of the Gatehouse, one of the matrons distributed them under the glare of our shift commander.

Since ADS "Arnold" told us that days off were rescinded, I showed up for picket duty on Thursday. However, union president "Everett" told me that no one was losing days off and that I could go home if I wanted. The entire situation was too distasteful for me to waste my free time carrying a picket sign, so I went home. On Friday, I received a call from a co-worker telling me the strike was over and that we were returning to work, but that was my other day off and I took advantage of it, going back to work on Saturday. When I investigated the aftermath of the strike to find out what was gained or lost, I was told that a judge had intervened, called the strike illegal and planned to fine AFSCME for each day it continued. When the union leaders were given this decision, they terminated the job action and called it a "wildcat strike," blaming the membership; even though AFSCME had instigated the work stoppage! How did I benefit from this event? I lost three days' pay, three days' seniority and had my official start date set back from June 6 to June 9, 1976. Thanks, AFSCME!

I became part of a fairly close-knit group of officers on the 4-12 shift from my first day with them till I changed to the 8-4 shift in March of 1978. Many of us relaxed with an adult beverage at The Clonmel Arms, a popular after-hours watering hole, played softball against other shifts, and bowled together for recreation. I was a member of the short-lived institution target shooting team which performed fairly well against other corrections and police departments, but the organization apparently suffered an overdose of apathy and competition was discontinued.

I knew of three other officers hired "off the street" prior to the restart of the Department of Correction Training Academy. In July of 1976, Officer "Gold" joined the 4-12 shift; in August, "Dominic" was added; and "Jim" started in September. I developed interesting relationships with all of them. "Gold" was a military veteran who was friendly and pleasurable to work with. He was eventually promoted through the ranks at an unusually rapid rate, a consequence of which was a noticeable change in his disposition. When I first saw "Dominic" sitting alone on a Gatehouse bench waiting for roll call, I gave him a friendly greeting. He responded with a silent scowl. I got the impression that we were going to bump heads before our careers were over; more on these two characters later in the text.

That fall I had my first encounter with an inmate disciplinary infraction. I was paired with new Officer "Jim" and was showing him how to perform a security check of the CSD building before locking its doors when we observed a convict picking up something from behind a piano in the auditorium. As we approached, I ordered him to stop, but he ran for the exit. "Jim" and I pursued him but instead of splitting up when we left the building, we both ran to the left, not knowing the inmate had gone right. I thought we had lost him, but we saw him running past another officer on the Quad and turning a corner.

Unfortunately, that officer didn't stop him. We had seen the inmate throw his package into a trash can and our resulting search found it to be an assortment of illegal drugs. We tracked him to Unit 1-3, the House Officer identified him for us, and we apprehended the felon in his room. After notifying the shift commander, he ordered us to escort the inmate to the segregation unit to be locked up pending investigation. "Jim" and I remained good friends throughout our careers and were active together in support of the new independent union years later.

On a snowy Christmas Day night of 1976 an inmate disturbance began at the women's facility, MCI Framingham. I and several of Norfolk's 4-12 officers were held over in the event we were needed to support those in Framingham. Our shift commander divided us into two teams, one led by Supervisor "Bob," and the other by Senior "George D." We were each handed a bag containing a gas mask, helmet and baton and waited impatiently to be deployed. Most, if not all of us had never received riot control training so we were told simply to "take down" any inmate that resisted us. Thankfully, at 1am, we were sent home after being notified that the Framingham fracas was under control.

The following year, 4-12 Supervisor "Chris" asked "Rhino" and me together if we would volunteer to join the newly created Tactical Team, specifically trained to respond to inmate disturbances. Members were required to be on-call 24 hours a day and to immediately report to the prison when notified that the team was being activated. "Rhino" declined without comment. I explained to "Chris" that I would comply with whatever was required of me while I was on duty, but I would **not** be available to sit by a telephone, drop whatever I was doing on my off time, just to confront disorderly convicts.

The first time I was assigned to "The Sixes" I was told to patrol the Quad, keep the inmates from congregating, and check on the House Officers in that area. I noticed one of them standing outside his unit, staring up at the sky, learned that his first name was the same as mine, so as I passed him I said, "Hi, Joe, how's it going?" He didn't acknowledge me; just kept staring upwards. I made another round of the Quad, walked up to him again to ask how he was doing but he still ignored me. On my third approach, I spoke to him once more and he responded, "I don't talk to 'temps!'" **What?** Because he was a permanent officer and I was still temporary, he wouldn't even **talk** to me? I thought Correction Officers were supposed to have some kind of camaraderie on the job! What difference did Civil Service status make? I walked away from him muttering, "Well, I don't talk to assholes!"

For a time, we 4-12 officers were placed on a six-month assignment rotation as a means of familiarizing us with the assortment of details on that shift. Most of us were comfortable knowing where we would work each day for that length of time. On occasion, I was assigned to the third floor RB, where I had received my "baptism of fire" on the first day of training. There were only three officers there during that shift and our responsibilities consisted simply of serving the evening meal, escorting a nurse on medication rounds, and keeping the tier quiet. An inmate "houseman" prepared the food trays and tended to the kitchen, while another was a janitor who cleaned the tier. It was disturbing to find that these two were pedophiles and convicted child-killers who were being held in protective custody but allowed out of their cells to work.

One of the particular responsibilities when assigned to "The Deuces" and monitoring the Mainline Kitchen was to search areas of the service tunnels beneath the institution for hidden contraband. Officers occasionally discovered containers of "home brew," a form of alcoholic beverage, hidden in certain areas.

Inmates who had access to canned fruit and juices would mix them with bread and place jugs of the concoction in steam-heated crevices, allowing them to ferment over time. A couple of months into my career I made my first "home brew" discovery, a noxious liquid made from ketchup, of all things! After filing my incident report, I disposed of that nasty mixture post haste! I could not imagine any inmate craving alcohol so much that he would have consumed something like this.

Briefly on the 4-12, there was some uneasiness surrounding the procedures we followed when counting inmates in their housing units at 10pm and 11pm. Supervisor "Manuel" addressed the shift one night and claimed that he and Superintendent "Michael" had noticed that we were not following protocol while counting. Our method was to have the backup officer open a corridor gate for the officer making the count, lock the gate when he finished and then open the next one. As a change, Supervisor "Manuel" ordered us to lock each counting officer *inside* a corridor while he made his count, instead of leaving the gate open. This was not only an extremely dangerous position in which to place the counting officer, it was nonsensical. If inmates wanted to attack officers or take them hostage, they could do so the second that the grilled gate was opened. An officer trapped inside a locked corridor would be in extreme danger and was better served having an opportunity to escape. We did not follow "Manuel's" order that night, but we were more deliberate than usual in completing the counts. One rookie officer did lock a veteran inside during a count and was severely reprimanded by his partners. We returned to our original procedure from then on after discovering that "Manuel" had taken it upon himself to issue this order. When some of us questioned the superintendent about the change, he told us he had nothing to do with it. Neither of them had observed our procedures because *no* counts had been taken yet! "Manuel" eventually left for the Day Shift, where his reputation preceded him, and ultimately retired, as far as I know.

The most bizarre assignment on the 4-12 shift was having to drive two inmate "trustees" to the prison's sewage treatment plant outside the walls; the "filter beds." Their jobs were to operate the machinery and circulate the waste twice over a short period of time. In between "stirrings," the officer would stay in a shack with the inmates while they ate a snack and enjoyed some time with a large group of feral cats that had made a home there.

I kept as alert as possible during my turn at this detail because I could envision how easy it would be for these inmates to assault me, steal the state vehicle, and escape if they so desired, especially since I was unarmed.

My least favorite post was always the prison Hospital because of the unpleasant nature of such an environment. Officers supervised inmate patients and provided security for the medical staff on the second floor. The doctors and nurses were pleasant and professional for the most part, but the inmates could be very unnerving, especially ones confined in a four-cell lockup area for mental health problems. It was exceedingly rare, but more than once I witnessed a nurse behaving overly friendly to an inmate. One nurse was reportedly terminated for engaging in a personal relationship with an inmate. She was alleged to have visited him frequently, and later married him!

For a short time, the third floor of the Hospital contained a diet kitchen area for inmates; yeah, you read right, a "diet kitchen" for convicts! A professional dietician supervised inmate cooks as they prepared specially prescribed meals for a few residents who ate in a general dining room. However, "underboss Enrico" was again treated as an exception. A few of his "soldiers" created special Italian dishes and arranged a separate restaurant-like setting for him and a select group of compatriots. The only thing missing was the Chianti!

It was in this diet kitchen that I observed my first obscene waste of food. One night the cooks made three large inserts of macaroni and cheese, but barely used one to feed the all the inmate diners. When the meal ended, I watched an inmate throw the entire contents of one of the inserts into the food waste barrel. As he prepared to dump the third, I stopped him, filled a separate container with as much macaroni as possible, and brought it to the OIC for my fellow officers to enjoy. DOC policy at the time forbade staff from eating inmate food and insisted any excess be disposed of, at taxpayers' expense, but I was patently offended by such horrible waste.

The administration also allowed a number of inmate "clubs" to be formed and permitted members to have regular functions in the old visiting room; more liberal "prison reform" gone berserk! A few other officers and I controlled the Ad Building Gate area and monitored an "Italian-American banquet" one evening. These inmates were allowed to have visitors join them in a feast of gourmet Italian cuisine while we watched over them.

Towards the end of the function, "underboss Enrico" ordered containers of lasagna, roast beef, and orange sherbet brought to the Ad Building and told his underlings, "I want all these officers fed." One of his lackeys was a notorious organized crime figure, also a "camp co-chairman," who strenuously objected to giving us the food, but "Enrico" just pointed and said, "Do it!" The cleanup crew actually gave one of the officers a bag of prime rib bones to take home for his dog! Norfolk was not called a "country club" prison for nothing!

Two Block: Units 2-1, 2-2, 2-3

Snowed In!

For the first twenty months of my career I honed my skills through a continuance of on-the-job training and became familiar with the various job requirements on the 4-12 shift. The more experienced officers turned out to be very cooperative and helpful, something that was less prevalent on the other shifts. I married in October of 1977 and my wife and I expected our first child later the next year. In between, though, the New England area was pummeled by the infamous Blizzard of '78 in February. I lived less than five miles from the prison, but the commute that first afternoon of the storm was treacherous.

The 4-12 shift was not surprisingly understaffed because of the weather, but there was no overtime draft to hold anyone from the 8-4 shift. As my fellow   4-12 officers and I entered the institution, the Day Shift hit the exit doors like a thundering herd of buffalo. They couldn't head home fast enough. Little did we know how long we'd be confined to the prison by the overwhelming storm.

We performed as many functions as possible for our shift in what amounted to emergency conditions, and then were told we all had to stay for the next shift to continue making the hourly inmate counts. The snow drifts kept growing and made patrolling unreasonably difficult, but the 4-12 pressed on. Our ADS shift commander and supervisors were very conscious of the difficulties we incurred and made sure we received food and rest when required. Their leadership was much appreciated. However, the same could not be said for those who oversaw the 12-8 shift.

Normally, the inmate counts from 12-8am were scheduled to commence at specific times and the numbers were to be called in to the Gatehouse control room within a few minutes of completion. With the blizzard worsening and the counting officers growing more tired, we weren't particularly worried about watching the clock, just completing our tasks. Besides, with several feet of snow accumulated already, it would not be an optimal time for any inmate to attempt an escape over the wall. He'd be lucky to even **make** it to the wall! The Midnight Shift commanders, ADS "Mush" and Supervisor "Norm," made timed rounds to check on their officers. "Norm" stopped by our base unit around 2am,

glared at us, said nothing, and then left. A couple of hours later, "Mush" paid a visit and also gave us no real recognition. He simply stood there watching. My two partners headed upstairs a few minutes later than the expected start time and "Mush" suddenly shouted, "My God, you haven't started the count yet?" We were all too tired to respond or argue with him and said nothing as he exited the unit. All we could do was shake our heads at his concern more with timeliness than with his officers' well-being. While the 4-12 commanders were as reasonable as they could be to the overworked officers, "Mush" and "Norm" couldn't have cared less and gave us nothing but condescension.

Our depleted 4-12 shift was obviously going to remain at the facility for a while longer. A few scattered officers made their way to work in the morning despite the snow drifts, a declared state of emergency, and barely passable roads.

After completing our 16-hour shift, some of us asked 12-8 Gatehouse Senior "Don" if we could go home. He said that we could leave if we were able to dig our cars out of the snow.

A few officers grabbed shovels from inmate trustees working outside and spent most of the day freeing their cars, while the rest of us simply located our buried vehicles and retired to common areas in the upper floors of the Gatehouse to get some sleep before returning to work at 4pm. We shared some "war stories" with co-workers and found that my counting crews weren't the only ones disrespected by the Midnight Shift commanders. Officer "Dapper" told us that Supervisor "Norm" had given his three-man team a significant amount of grief regarding the timeliness of their rounds, and "Dapper" became so enraged he threatened to throw "Norm" into a snow bank. When ADS "Mush" later checked on them, he glared, pointed to the inmate coffee pot that the officers had turned on early and shouted, "What's that?" "Dapper" replied, "It's nice, hot coffee, you want some?" "Mush" didn't respond to the question, but pointed to the portable radio the officers were listening to in the unit office and snapped, "What's *that*?" "Dapper's" fellow officers were astonished when he replied, "What are you, fucking stupid? It's a new invention called a radio! You turn it on and get music and news; now get the fuck out of here!" The ADS left in a huff, and he and "Norm" filed disciplinary incident reports against "Dapper." Not to be outdone, in fine Midnight Shift character, Gatehouse Senior "Don" reported that the officers who had managed to extricate their cars and leave had done so without permission. A couple of 4-12 officers and I overheard this lie and explained to 4-12 Supervisor "Chris" what actually occurred. After the superintendent was made aware of the way the 12-8 commanders were treating the 4-12 officers, he dismissed all the negative reports against them. At least *he* showed some character and concern for his men.

The blizzard kept us confined at the prison and I worked my double shifts as expected. At least I was free to walk around as much as possible, unlike the poor tower officers who were unable to be relieved because of the drifts that blocked their doorways. Even though they had water and toilet facilities on site and were able to obtain food by lowering buckets on ropes to officers on the outside, they had to remain in the towers for several consecutive shifts until the snow was removed and replacements could arrive. After my first long shift, I slept on a couch in the roll call room. I walked through the Gatehouse a few hours later and noticed Superintendent "Michael" inside the control room. I asked our old pal "Don" if I could speak to the boss, but he wouldn't allow it.

However, after managing to get his attention, the superintendent approached me. I explained to him that I lived only a few miles from the prison and asked if I could go home, get some real sleep, a change of clothes and decent food. He told me I could, as long as I returned and worked my expected sixteen hours. I agreed, thanked him kindly and glanced to see "Don" giving me quite the dirty look as I departed.

By a stroke of luck, my neighbors had managed to uncover my pregnant wife's car from a snow pile and she was able to drive me home. There were no other vehicles on the snow-packed roads at the time, just folks walking or cross-country skiing, so we first made our way to the nearest convenience store. The vending machines at the prison had long since been emptied, and as an act of good will, I bought as many soft drinks, snacks, and cigarettes as I could afford to give to my fellow officers. My wife volunteered to deliver the supplies while I slept, and I told her to make sure she gave them only to Supervisor "Chris," who I trusted to distribute them fairly. I was greeted very thankfully by my shift-mates when I returned.

All the officers who worked long hours and remained at the prison for several days were compensated adequately, not just with overtime pay but credited with additional time off in the form of "snow days" to be used later.

The irony of the Blizzard of '78 situation was that if I had simply called the institution and stated that I was "trying to come in" but never made it, instead of

fighting my way through the storm, I still would have received the "snow days" even while staying home. Who knew? At least I picked up some nice overtime.

When the snow stopped falling, the cleanup process was a sight to behold. Inmates shoveled pathways to the various buildings behind the walls, and we made our rounds as if we were in a maze, unable to see over the snow piles. Front-end loaders removed the bulk of the white stuff, and eventually the orderly running of the institution was restored.

The Iconic "Gong!"

The Day Shift

Business at MCI Norfolk took place during weekdays on the 8-4, later 7-3 Day Shift. Most inmates went to their various work assignments, while others attended an assortment of education classes, religious services, or counseling sessions. Some inmates exercised at the indoor gym or outside on softball diamonds, jogging tracks, basketball courts, or weight lifting areas. (Sounds like really harsh punishment, eh?) Supply vehicles made deliveries, and clerical staff tended to treasury, personnel, and non-security issues. In March of 1978, several positions on the 8-4 shift became available, as a number of veteran officers accepted promotions, retired, or transferred elsewhere, and many of us on the 4-12 submitted bids for those slots. In the past, officers needed perhaps ten years of seniority to join the Day Shift, but now, with only twenty-two months on the job, I won an 8-4 bid with Wednesdays and Thursdays off, and joined about a dozen of my 4-12 comrades in changing shifts. We all were delighted to be working during the day for a change, but ADS "Arnold" was less than thrilled. Prior to our departure, he angrily accused us of wrecking his 4-12 shift, even though bid changes were regular occurrences.

It was certainly not *our* fault for leaving, and new officers would be filling our vacancies. He couldn't have expected us to stay on his shift for our entire careers!

There was an unwritten understanding back in the late 1970s that some officers with many years of experience received the same assignments each day. I was of the impression that newer officers were expected to put in their time, learn the various routines, and then settle into more comfortable or less physically taxing positions. On the 4-12 shift, seasoned officers were regulars in Towers One and Three. When I joined the Day Shift, veterans worked One and Three Towers each day they were on duty as well. The Gatehouse control room, some yard posts and a few other interior positions also were manned by regularly assigned officers. The newer 8-4 members were rotated through the assortment of jobs in order to gain experience.

During my first stint on the 8-4 shift, the Inner Perimeter Security team was created and open positions were made available to interested officers. The

superintendent was authorized to assign a certain percentage of the security force to areas of his choosing, bypassing seniority, and all the IPS slots were designated as "Superintendent's Picks." The initial mission of IPS was to search inmates, crawl through housing units and attics, and look inside other buildings for contraband. The team commanders were chosen by the superintendent and they, in turn, recommended other officers to complete the group. I was one of many officers who submitted a bid for an IPS position, but was not accepted. A standing not-so-funny joke at the time was that a person needed to be from Milford, Massachusetts, to be on the IPS team because of apparent nepotism or cronyism. I was not from Milford.

As time progressed, IPS officers continued their search routines, but they began morphing into more of an "Internal Affairs" investigative force, scrutinizing employees as well as targeting inmates. The superintendent even created a "Special Investigator" position on that team to address staff security issues.

One of the more desirable places to work was in the Segregation Unit, third floor RB. Though it housed a variety of problematic inmates, the routine was quite simple for staff.

An inmate houseman and janitor prepared meals from food received by dumbwaiter from the Mainline Kitchen and then cleaned the tier. Breakfast trays were distributed by officers.

Convicts confined to the right side cells received showers and mopped their cells on one day, and the other side did so the following day. Those who desired one hour exercise periods were escorted to one of four large chain-link cages on the building's roof. These tasks were often completed before noon. Lunch would be served, and then activity was limited to Hospital visits, dispensing medication, transfers and the like. The unit senior at the time, "Al," along with some regularly assigned veteran officers would ensure that all inmates were secure and the corridor was locked down. The crew member with the least amount of seniority was forced to remain inside the control post, operate the various doors and gates, answer the phone and make log book entries, while the others played cards on the tier. This practice became so commonplace that officers practically begged to be assigned to the RB. We essentially worked a half-day for a full day's pay. What a racket! As long as the inmates behaved themselves and caused no disturbances, the shifts went by like clockwork.

This particular routine obviously could not last indefinitely because many different officers were part of the assignment rotation. I never experienced any

significant problems working in the RB back then, never engaged in any major fracases with inmates or staff, and never witnessed any serious injuries. However, one episode served to sour several officers on how this unit was being operated. My old pal "Rhino" regularly engaged in late night entertainment on his off time and was very tired come the morning. He commuted to work by carpool and usually slept on the way in. One driver even placed a mattress in the back of his station wagon for "Rhino" to sleep on. Sometimes he would report to his post and find a place to nod off; a very dangerous practice. When he did so in the RB, the other officers had to pick up his slack, with four doing the work of five. Senior "Al" never objected to this behavior. One particular day, "Rhino" reported to the third floor RB, proceeded into an empty cell, and fell asleep on the bed. The four of us who were awake complained to "Al" and demanded he rectify this problem. The only step he took was to lock the cell door to hide "Rhino's" sleeping when a supervisor made an inspection of the tier. It appeared that "Al" was afraid of this weight-lifter because I couldn't imagine any other officer receiving such bizarre accommodations. None of us mentioned this incident again, but I was rarely assigned to the RB after that. The carefree days of card playing were pretty much coming to an end.

The rotating assignments found me on the Quad again one day, escorting a civilian telephone repairman through a few of the housing units. My responsibility was to stay with him, providing security while he worked near inmates. Suddenly, I heard an emergency radio call for reaction to an assault near my location. Normally I would have responded but since I wasn't supposed to leave this man, I called the OIC senior for instructions. He advised me to remain with the repairman until he left the facility. I only witnessed the aftermath of the disturbance. One Hispanic inmate had mixed urine and feces in a milk container and threw it at another Hispanic, who retaliated by stabbing his assailant. The Quad became a crime scene of blood and human waste, but other officers were able to quickly subdue the combatants and restore order.

In the summer of 1978, MCI Norfolk's inmates went "on strike." The leaders of the demonstration actually refused to allow other inmates to work, except for those in the Mainline Kitchen to keep food being served and Hospital orderlies to care for inmate patients. Theories abounded as to the grievances surrounding this action, but they were probably an amalgam of everything inmates normally complain about. At least there was no destruction of property nor any injuries that I knew of. Correctional employees continued their routines but

management decided to hold over a number of volunteer officers to support each shift in case violence broke out at the prison. I accumulated a significant amount of overtime pay simply by agreeing to stay an extra four hours, playing pool, cards, or napping in the roll call room.

After too many days of this disorder, the DOC finally had enough of the nonsense. From a number of observation areas, officers compiled information and identified instigators of the "strike," and the department ordered a morning incursion into the prison to remove around 100 inmates for transfer to out-of-state facilities. Norfolk did not have a special weapons team at the time, so armed Massachusetts State Police officers lined the Quad while Correction Officer tactical teams apprehended the inmates and brought each one to the Administration Building.

I was part of a dressed extraction team of 8-4 and drafted 12-8 officers from the previous night, kept on standby in case any RB inmates created a disturbance and had to be dealt with, but those inmates were quiet during the entire ship-out. We were then instructed to have two officers from our team alternate taking each handcuffed inmate out of the Ad Building after he received a medical examination and lay him on the grass in the "dead zone" in front of Five Tower. The inmates were watched over by a pair of officers in the tower, a few correction counselors, and at least one armed state police officer with a K-9 unit until they were transferred.

The West Field

As the operation progressed, the unfortunate 12-8 officers had been on duty for more than sixteen hours and were becoming exhausted. We asked a few different supervisors to allow the 12-8 crew to either be relieved or given some rest. Most of them had little compassion for the officers' situation, but one finally arranged for them to go home, as they were no longer needed.

The exercise was completed quickly and efficiently without a noticeable problem, and there was never a repeat "strike" during my years at Norfolk.

Into The Night

My career sailed along from 1978 to 1980, but my personal life didn't fare as well. After three years of marriage, I was forced to divorce my wife, but I retained custody of our two-year-old son. We were living together with my elderly aunt in her home for a short time, caring for her in exchange for room and board, but suddenly I became a single parent. I could not expect my aunt to accommodate the needs of a toddler by herself, so I had no choice but to change my work hours and days off, having enough seniority to win a bid on the 10pm to 6am shift with weekends off. This way, I could take my son to a babysitter, sleep from 8am to 2pm, bring him home and tend to all the requirements of my new family arrangement. I would put him to bed around 8pm and my aunt would at least be in the house in case an emergency arose.

Since the job requirements on that shift were exclusively to count inmates each hour, two with the 4-12 shift and six with the 12-8 shift, I never expected to encounter many problems, knowing that most of the prisoners would be sleeping. It wasn't long before I was proven wrong.

Counting inmates during daylight hours was done during the three scheduled mealtimes when most of them were congregated in small areas. House Officers tabulated the numbers in their respective units, while inmates working in the Mainline Kitchen, Hospital or other areas outside the housing units were counted by officers monitoring those sites. From 10pm to 6am, the convicts were confined to their units, and teams of three officers alternated counting them

each hour. The corridors containing individual rooms were closed off by locked wire gates, with the exception of the Six Block units where the floor levels were open and beds were arranged barracks-style in large enclosures. Protocol dictated that one officer would conduct the count; a backup officer controlled the keys, opening and closing each gate while watching for potential problems; and the third member remained in the unit office near the telephone in case trouble occurred. Counting inmates in relative darkness using a flashlight could be unnerving at times, as we never knew if a prisoner was hiding somewhere, planning an assault, or preparing to cause some kind of disturbance. Our mandate was to see "living, breathing flesh," which meant that we were forced to tap on an observation window or knock on a room door to force a sleeper completely covered by sheets and blankets to show himself.

Early in my time on that shift, I was conducting a count and discovered one inmate inside another's room. Institutional rules prohibited such behavior after the units were locked for the evening, though there was little an officer could do to prevent it. In this instance, one inmate was hastily pulling up his pants while the other was lying on his bed semi-clothed. There was little doubt that they were engaging in unauthorized sexual conduct, plus the inmate that did not reside in that particular room was out of bounds; both infractions. I wrote disciplinary reports on each one, noting the particular violations, and submitted them to the 12-8 shift commander.

The next evening, ADS "Mush" confronted me and said he had dismissed the reports, claiming that I couldn't charge the inmates with unauthorized sexual behavior unless I actually "caught them in the act!" The fact that one of them was out of bounds didn't matter to "Mush," either, and it appeared that he would rather have quiet and undisturbed shifts than encourage his officers to uphold the rules of the institution.

One evening a while later, I was assigned to the "Sixes" and upon trying to enter Unit 6-1 for the 10pm count, the 4-12 officers and I discovered that inmates had barricaded the door with trash barrels. The Six Block units were the only ones that were designed as open dormitories, giving inmates freedom of movement within the buildings. We called for assistance and forced our way into the unit, where we found that inmates had coated door handles with petroleum jelly as well. Without warning, one of my partners, a big Scotsman named "Vic," began picking up the barrels and throwing them into the hallway and the inmate dining

room, creating a noisy mess. I couldn't fault him for his anger, but I had no idea what response his actions would bring.

Supervisor "Jack" arrived on scene and asked what had happened. "Vic" told him that inmates had scattered the trash. My other partner and I stayed away from the conversation. More officers responded and "Jack" ordered the inmate janitor and houseman, who lived on the first floor, to clean up the debris and wipe off the doorknobs. "Vic" was forced to write the incident report, and all was quiet for the rest of the night. His behavior would have been more humorous if the situation hadn't been so serious.

Later in 1981, I was again counting the Six Block with two 4-12 officers when we smelled a distinct odor coming from the first floor rooms of Unit 6-1 and found the inmate houseman smoking marijuana. One of my partners called for a supervisor who then assigned two other officers to escort the inmate to be locked up in the RB. I searched the inmate's room, confiscated the marijuana evidence, and submitted it with a disciplinary report.

When his hearing was scheduled, the inmate requested my presence, as was his prerogative. Since I was working from 10pm to 6am, I was never on duty during regular institutional business hours, but the Disciplinary Officer left me an envelope containing a notice to appear, posted in the Gatehouse control room. My strict routine required that I complete a shift and head home to care for my family. For me to return to the prison or change shifts would seriously interfere with that schedule.

I explained the situation *in writing* to the Disciplinary Officer, and received no further notifications. A week or so later, I received a letter ordering me to appear at another disciplinary hearing....this time with *me* as the defendant! I couldn't begin to understand what rule I allegedly violated.

I had no choice but to go home after my shift, take my son to his babysitter, and head back to Norfolk for the hearing. I appeared before two ADS shift commanders who told me that I was charged with refusing to appear at the disciplinary hearing for the inmate I had cited for smoking marijuana. They claimed that the Disciplinary Officer had given me an opportunity to change my shift to cooperate with the process and accused me of declining. I explained to the board members that I was never given that option, nor did I refuse to change my shift, and clearly indicated to the Disciplinary Officer that family issues prevented me from attending. Since I had heard nothing more about the matter, I considered it closed. Come to find out, the disciplinary hearing based

on my report was conducted in my absence, the hearing officer found the inmate guilty of marijuana possession and gave him an appropriate sanction. Meanwhile, *I* was "tried" and found guilty of failing to report for an inmate's disciplinary hearing....the date and time of which I had *never been told!* I ended up receiving a letter of reprimand which was placed in my personnel file. This travesty made me start re-evaluating my future in this correctional system.

The "Deuces" and the "Sixes"

Return To Daylight

After functioning as a single parent and pounding out a living on the 10-6 shift for more than a year, I finally caught a break. A judge finalized my divorce and awarded me full custody of my son, and I was able to enter the dating scene again. I met a wonderful woman named Debbie, my soon-to-be best friend, life partner, and new mother for my son. Shortly afterwards, we received a significant shock when my aunt died at home unexpectedly and my son and I became the only residents in her house. I no longer had overnight adult supervision for my son, so Debbie volunteered to move in with us to fill that void. She also worked a full-time job so I still needed a babysitter to care for him during the day while I slept at home. Debbie soon chose to sacrifice her job in

order to become a regular homemaker and mother.

I purchased my aunt's house out of probate and we had a good roof over our heads. However, Debbie felt uneasy sleeping alone with only my toddler son in the house at night, so it was time for me to change shifts again.

I managed to secure an 8-4 spot with Wednesdays and Thursdays off. It was preferable to work weekends during the day and be home each night than to have the weekend off but be stuck on the night shift. Some notable changes occurred shortly after my return.

"Bill C" had risen through the officer ranks to become superintendent. He solicited a survey among the employees asking if they would prefer changing the work hours from 8-4 and so on back one hour, to 7-3, etc., with the 10-6 shift expected to be melded into the 11-7. MCI Walpole, situated a couple of miles from MCI Norfolk, already utilized the 7-3 shift times, and the difference of one hour in our respective shifts created an overlap of extra officers who could assist in the event of emergencies at either institution. That made sense. The majority response to the survey was to maintain the established work hours. The superintendent, however, ignored the results and changed our shift hours to the Walpole model. It appeared that "Bill C" had made up his mind prior to asking for popular opinion, so all we could do was wonder why he bothered in the first place and make the adjustment to start working an hour earlier.

A more acceptable change was that of replacing the old dark green and khaki uniforms with new blue shirts, trousers, jackets and appropriate accessories. We now looked less like bus drivers and more like police officers. Even the House Officers eventually changed to wearing the new uniforms.

At some point in the 1980s, the Department of Correction was transferred from the governmental agency of Health and Human Services to Public Safety, where it belonged. This change allowed the DOC to be included with State Police and related organizations when negotiating collective bargaining agreements with the state legislature.

The institutional chain of command originally held the titles of Assistant Deputy Superintendent, Supervisor, Senior and Correction Officer. I believe it happened prior to the uniform changes, but ultimately the higher rankings were re-named Captain, Lieutenant, and Sergeant, and along with those ranks came the

appropriate military-style insignias.

In May of 1983, Debbie and I married and remain happily so to this day. My son now had two parents to raise him through a normal childhood, and our daughter was born in 1985. I managed to improve my days off to Fridays and Saturdays and once again, my career seemed to be moving on an even keel. I still received random assignments, from tower duty to yard supervision, the Hospital, assorted interior building posts and an occasional transportation detail, but my preferred positions were the RB or a tower. I always felt that those two prison assignments were the only sensible ones. The RB officers kept the felons secured in their cells, while the tower officers prevented potential escapees from scaling the walls. The rest of the operation was a plethora of exercises in social experimentation and the progressive notion of "restorative justice." These were mutations from the leftist prison reform movement which began in the 1960s. At least the placement into Public Safety from Human Services shifted prison control away from the "social worker" mentality and closer to the security approach....or so we thought!

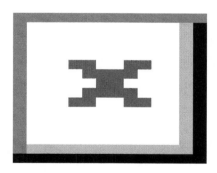

Two Tower

As the 1980s progressed, I was more frequently assigned to the RB than any other post. The three levels of this segregation unit received a general overhaul, with the RDC program on the first floor being transformed into a protective custody cellblock, housing mostly sex offenders. It was re-named the Norfolk Reintegration Unit (NRU); more word-play. The two upper floors were used for disciplinary confinement.

From my first day on the job, I became familiar with the mechanisms used to open and close cell doors in the RB. They were complex designs of horizontal metal bands running above the cell doors. Disengaging a lever, or pin, inside a control station released the door's lock, and then the officer in the post would manually rotate a large metal wheel to physically pull the door open or push it closed. It was possible to open some or all of the cell doors at once, but as time went on, incidents of malfunctions increased, requiring attention by the locksmith and maintenance personnel. The institution finally procured a contract to electrify the doors and control panels. Construction began on the first and third floors around the same time, with the second floor project being completed a while later.

During the transition between manual and electric operations, cell doors had to be secured by welded chain links and padlocks, requiring officers to unlock each cell individually. It was a slow process and potentially dangerous in the event of a fire or large-scale disturbance, but fortunately none ever happened. I did, however, earn a lasting nickname after an incident on the second floor RB.

The cell doors were not sealed tightly while padlocked. Inmates were able to crack them slightly, just far enough to throw something onto the tier. In addition to being able to leave their cells for exercise and to shower, they were allowed to use a pay telephone that was mounted on the tier wall. One particular day, I escorted an elderly inmate named "Irving" to the phone. He was an infamous child molester, given protective custody, despised by staff and convicts alike, and constantly berated by other felons. When he finished the call and was returning to his cell, another inmate opened his own door an inch and threw water at the pedophile.

He soaked the old man but splashed a considerable amount on me, yelling, "Ha, ha, it's piss!" As "Irving" hurriedly waddled his way back to the safety of his cell, I examined my uniform to see if the wetness was indeed urine. The inmate who assaulted us was laughing hysterically. After locking "Irving" in his cell, I opened the assailant's door in order to deal with his assault. He apologized to me, claiming that the liquid was only water and that his target was the child molester. I physically dragged him from his room, moved him to a more secure "rip-out" cell and ordered him to undress for a strip search. By this time, my fellow officers were reveling in my indignation and joined in the laughter. The inmate stripped down to his underwear and stood there chuckling, so I shouted at him, "Drop those drawers!" My partner, Officer "Dapper," immediately exclaimed, "Go get 'em, Joe Studd!"

That moniker stuck with me for the rest of my career....and beyond!

I remember one other incident that enraged me more than having a felon throw water on me. For a short time, some transferred inmates were held in segregation until correction counselors screened them for placement in general population. One day, the RB sergeant directed me to escort black convicted murderer "Weldon" from the lockup to Unit 3-1. I let him out the rear door of the building and through a chain-link gate located near that housing unit. "Weldon" was serving a life sentence for the brutal robbery, rape, and murder of a young, white, female nurse in Boston. Upon recognizing him, a couple of other black inmates shouted, "Yo, Yo, Weldon," and dashed up to shake his hand and hug him. This filthy animal destroyed a woman's life, but he was celebrated by his friends! I wish a pox on all the bleeding-heart voters and politicians who outlawed capital punishment!

During my years walking the floors of the RB, the unit was supervised by several different lieutenants. Over time, some accepted promotions, voluntarily transferred or were reassigned by prison management. One thing was certain; their leadership abilities and demeanors ran the gamut from respectability to utter incompetence and affected the performances of the officers in their charge. Lieutenant "B" was the first notable example of ineptitude. His mission seemed to be more focused on finding fault with officers and coddling inmates than maintaining the orderly running of the unit. One morning, a young inmate on the second floor began a disturbance merely to get attention. In addition to pounding his cell door and screaming obscenities, he purposely clogged his cell's toilet, causing it to overflow.

I was unable to access a valve to shut off the water, so I ordered the inmate to put his hands through the food slot to be placed in handcuffs. He complied, I cuffed him, and he sat on his bed. All that was left was to gather a couple of officers for support, remove the inmate from the cell and stop the flooding. Lt. "B" then responded to the fracas and told us not to remove the inmate because he had called for an extraction team to physically subdue him. I explained to the lieutenant that I had already restrained the inmate and he was willing to exit the cell on his own, but Lt. "B" gave the officers on the scene a direct order to stand down. Meanwhile, water continued to flow onto the tier, down the stairs and into the first floor.

Some of that floor's officers rushed upstairs and demanded to know why we weren't containing the inmate and the flood. We explained that Lt. "B" directly ordered us not to proceed. The officers were understandably irate. Ultimately, an extraction team moved the inmate, the flooding was stopped and the cleanup had begun, but there was no way I was going to let the lieutenant's behavior go unreported.

After the morning duties were completed and lunch was served, the unit became quiet, the tier was secure, and my two co-workers were enjoying a break. Rather than submit an incident report to the superintendent, which I expected would be ignored, I began typing a letter to the AFSCME local union president, detailing the incident involving Lt. "B." On any other day, one could find Lt. "B" enjoying his noon meal in the staff dining room at this time, but as bad luck would have it, he wandered unexpectedly into my control post and said, "Hi, how's it going? What are you writing?" There I sat in front of a typewriter containing a report with Lt. "B's" name all over it, so I just removed the paper and told him politely that it was nothing. He insisted that I tell him what I was writing and I responded, respectfully again, that it was nothing that he needed to be concerned with. He then became angry and ordered me to give him the letter, but I refused, reiterating that it was a personal matter. Guess who *else* was about to be written up?

A few days later, I received a notice that I was the subject of another incident report and was ordered to report for a hearing. I appeared in front of two captains with whom I had good relationships. Lt. "B" was in the room as well. I had waived union representation because I felt the incident was insignificant.

Captain "Paul" chaired the hearing alongside Captain "Rich." He read the report into the record and asked to hear my version of the incident. After accurately explaining the circumstances, I emphasized my decision to file a report with the union rather than with the administration and asserted my right to do so, citing confidential business. Capt. "Paul" appeared to be understanding of the situation and more or less wanted to dismiss the case. Capt. "Rich," however, tried to find fault with my activity, asking, "Why did you use a state typewriter to conduct union activity?" "Why did you use state paper?" "Why did you use state time?" Good grief! In closing the hearing, Capt. "Paul" asked me if a letter of reprimand would be appropriate for my disobeying Lt. "B's" order, adding that I could petition the superintendent to have it expunged from my record in six months. I insisted that I should receive no discipline of any kind because I hadn't violated an order; I simply exercised my union rights. My "trial" was over and, not surprisingly, I received another letter of reprimand, chock full of untruths. At some point in the future I rebutted in writing the two letters I received during my career but never did request to have either of them removed. To me, they were badges of honor for standing on principle.

Capt. "Paul" continued to be friendly towards me for all the years we worked together. I never forgot that he was the first supervisor to encourage me to apply for promotion, and I don't think he ever forgot one enormous favor I did for him. While walking the Quad at the beginning of a shift one day, I spotted a large ring of keys lying on the pavement, in plain sight of hundreds of inmates. I took them to the OIC and found then-Lieutenant "Paul" suffering a panic attack, as he had accidentally dropped them on his way in. One can imagine his relief when I returned them to him, because those keys opened every lock inside the prison.

Capt. "Rich" was a sociable man for as long as I knew him, but he became a bit abrasive towards staff after being promoted. I attended one of his refresher training sessions during which he lectured the class about how we all had to maintain dedication and devotion to the job, and not to forget that the inmates were our priorities. He then barked, "Anyone who is here just for the pay and benefits should leave now!" I was the first of many who stood and headed for the door. We thought his comment was made in jest because pay and benefits were the **only** reasons we were Correction Officers.

Coddling of inmates was reserved for counselors and mental health professionals. If Capt. "Rich's" glare could have killed, we'd have all been vaporized!

Much to my surprise, as time passed, Lt. "B" and I eventually became good friends, though I never forgot, nor did I forgive him for the RB incident. He had been reassigned several times, apparently for ineffectiveness, and appeared to finally be coming to his senses. He seemed to change his perception of management and gravitated towards being an advocate for the new independent union. We were now common allies.

The routines on each floor of the RB were generally uneventful. Inmates were confined there for many reasons; protective custody, disciplinary infractions, transfers to and from other institutions, and violent behavior. But when disorder erupted, we officers earned our pay, and then some. Disturbances were most often instigated by incorrigible inmates, but occasionally, institution policy exacerbated the problems. When the first floor RB was called the Departmental Segregation Unit (DSU), problem inmates, usually from Walpole, were placed in a liberal, "prison reform-type" program designed to rehabilitate and reintroduce them to the general population. They received counseling, work assignments, and were given regular evaluations, but it's fair to say that the program was a complete failure, as it was scrapped after a few years. Incredibly, these inmates were allowed to have metal lockers inside their cells. The administration was more concerned about a convict's comfort than the obstacle a locker would create in the event an extraction team was required to remove him by force. Lt. "B" once responded to an inmate who was banging his door and smashing items inside his cell. He foolishly opened the door's food slot to talk to the inmate when a piece of the metal locker came flying out. Fortunately, the lieutenant wasn't injured, but his carelessness was quite telling.

For most of my time working in the RB, the residents were allowed to make purchases from a general store inside the prison called the "Inmate Canteen." It was bad enough that this market existed in the first place, as convicted felons certainly don't deserve any such perks while serving criminal sentences, but to allow segregated inmates to receive grocery items from a store was absurd. At times, those with enough money in their "canteen accounts" filled their cells with cases of soft drink cans, easily used as weapons, as well as glass jars and petroleum jelly which could impede or injure officers entering their cells. One inmate threw an empty glass mayonnaise jar out of his food slot, barely missing me and shattering on the tier. The administration prudently removed the "Inmate Canteen" towards the end of my career.

MCI Walpole 10-Block inmate "Eric" was often violent and notoriously adept at picking locks and escaping from handcuffs. He was being held on the second floor when the cell doors were secured with padlocks. One day he managed to open his lock, walked down the tier, threw it between the bars into the secure control post where officers were sitting, demanded to see the superintendent, and then went back into his cell.

That same inmate later coerced several others on the second floor RB to join him in "ripping out." They smashed their cells' porcelain toilets and sinks and kept pounding on their doors. Two extraction teams were required to remove and restrain the inmates involved, but only the instigator resisted, receiving multiple injuries. When the superintendent finally visited "Eric" and witnessed the abrasions and lacerations he received fighting the extraction team, the inmate smiled and said, "I didn't think your guys had the heart to do this!"

Another time, several RB officers and I were called to bring waist chains and leg irons in response to a disturbance inside the prison yard. An inmate under the influence of an unknown intoxicant became assaultive and was resisting efforts to restrain him. We finally managed to shackle and carry him to the third floor RB. After securing him to the cell bed, another officer and I searched him and found a foul-smelling, plastic-wrapped substance in one of his pockets. I wrote an incident report and submitted it along with the evidence but never found out what the material was.

One inmate serving time for a sexual offense refused my order to leave his third floor cell to be transferred. Two other officers gave him similar orders but he wouldn't comply. The unit sergeant then came to assist us in removing the inmate when suddenly, he kicked the sergeant in the groin. Rather than walking out under his own power, we placed the inmate in handcuffs and leg irons and carried him out of the building. As he cried out for sympathy from other inmates, screaming that we were "killing him," all he received were insults and references to his crime from fellow convicts.

Despite the adrenalin-filled incidents that officers had to contend with, we made every effort to keep peace in the RB. We abided by departmental policies, gave segregated inmates items that they were entitled to, and diffused potential problems with reason and common sense, to the extent possible.

For a couple of years, I worked with three or four other officers regularly on the

second floor RB and we rarely encountered a problem we couldn't resolve. We didn't abuse the inmates, accommodated their needs without compromising security, and if giving them some leftover food or drink would keep them quiet, we took advantage of that simple effort. The inmates learned quickly that kindness was not to be mistaken for weakness, though. On the rare occasion that force had to be used to make an inmate comply with orders, we made sure it was not excessive.

In one instance, an Hispanic inmate named "Renaldo" was out of his cell for a shower but then refused my order to return. He pushed past me on the tier, shoving me with both hands, and said he was going to speak with the officer in the control post. Before I could react, Officer "Marc" suddenly appeared and tackled the inmate to the floor. He and I handcuffed the assailant and locked him in a special security cell. This was an excellent example of one officer responding quickly to assist another.

A week or so later, after receiving several disciplinary reports for an assortment of infractions, a transportation officer arrived to transfer "Renaldo" to MCI Bridgewater. The officer placed him in waist chains and leg irons and I helped him escort the inmate out of the institution. He complained constantly as we walked, not wanting to go to Bridgewater, but after we entered Post One on our way out of the RB, "Renaldo" started struggling, even though he was shackled. The transportation officer and I were forced to take him to the floor. The officer manning the post called for assistance, even though we didn't need any, and the next thing I knew, a half-dozen officers were piled on top of the inmate, the transportation officer and me. Four of us picked up "Renaldo" and forcibly carried him out to the transfer vehicle.

As I aged and had to deal with the increasingly nagging effects of two lower back injuries sustained at home, I asked to be excused from extraction team duty, fearing the possibility of aggravating old wounds. I had participated in many cell extractions over the years, and there were now plenty of younger, stronger officers available who were more capable than I. Instead of advancing with a team's protective shield or grappling with restraint equipment, I was assigned to be a videographer, responsible for recording extraction procedures. I was grateful for the change.

Inmate "David" was infamously problematic. He was aggressive, psychologically

disturbed, and never acclimated to the prison's general population, spending much of his incarceration in the segregation unit. "David" would regularly start banging his cell door, looking for attention, but it was often difficult to understand what he wanted. Correction counselors and prison mental health experts spent hours talking with him and trying to convince him to be cooperative, with little success. One particular day, after a few minutes of pounding his cell door, "David" decided to smear himself and the cell walls with his own feces. The shift commander ordered an extraction team to remove the inmate, take him to the prison Hospital for a shower, and then restrain him in a special cell there. "Lucky me" had the job of videotaping the event. The stench on the tier grew worse by the second, but at least I didn't have to dress in a protective suit and help carry this soiled convict to the hospital. The RB lieutenant had quite a difficult time soliciting inmate janitors to clean the mess in "David's" cell afterwards. It was damned certain that neither I nor any other officer would have done that job!

A female psychiatrist who was on scene tried to tell me that "David" was not crazy, just seeking attention. I pointed out to her that lower life forms do not normally cover themselves with their own waste, so how could she claim that this human being was not insane? No person in his right mind would ever commit such an act!

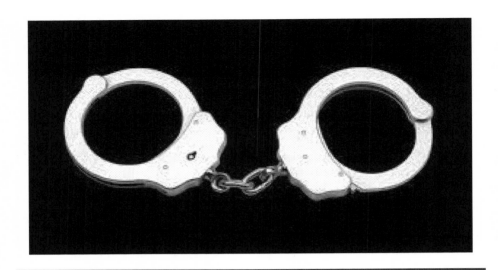

Banishment

Working in a segregation unit, especially for extended periods of time, can be understandably stressful for officers, but I still preferred that post to any other, with the exception of a tower. An officer had to be vigilant and alert on tower duty, not only to prevent escapees from scaling the wall but to monitor activity within prison yards and support fellow officers by reporting observations or, in worst case scenarios, providing armed protection in the event of inmate attacks. A tower offered freedom from inmate contact and unsavory interpersonal relationships, and an officer in that position earned the same salary as others without encountering many of the risks on the other side of the wall.

I worked two years on the second floor RB with a regular crew before being worked into a rotation of duties for a short time. It was sensible for officers to become familiar with every post in the institution, but the administration seemed to believe that stagnation resulted from long-term assignments. Line officers, however, showed that job performance consistency was more the case. In actuality, management's desire was to be able to control officers and keep them off balance through random, inconsistent placements. Shift commanders also used undesirable areas, such as the monotonous Five Tower routine, as posts that were perceived as "punishment" for some reason. Despite the stagnation theory, I was returned to the group of regular officers on the third floor RB and became a fixture there for nearly four years.

I was a stickler for rules and regulations and enforced them in the RB without overstepping any bounds. Some of these segregated convicts were quite ingenious in devising ways to hide contraband or pass it to each other, but I quickly discovered many of these attempts. They would make ropes out of torn bed sheets, tie cigarettes or other items to the ends, and either throw them down the tier or lower them through their outside windows to inmates on floors below. I regularly spotted such attempts, conducted cell searches, and confiscated unauthorized material, including dangerous sharpened implements. Needless to say, many inmates accused me of stealing their possessions and complained about me to the unit supervisor. My sergeant, however, had nothing but praise for my efforts.

The department then implemented six-month evaluations of all RB officers, insuring that their job performances were up to par and asking if they wanted to continue working there. A new supervisor, my one-time friend and carpool partner Lt.

"C," conducted these interviews. I told him that I was experiencing no problems and wanted to remain in the RB. My prior written evaluations were excellent and he acknowledged that I was doing a good job on the third floor. He hinted, though, that he thought I was looking "kind of tired," but I assured him I was fine.

A day or two later, I stood with my fellow RB officers at roll call exchanging small talk. The shift commander announced assignments for the day, but I wasn't included in the RB crew. Several officers turned to look at me, curiously surprised and wondering if I had done something to warrant removal from the RB. The captain placed me as a Quad officer. My good friend, Sgt. "Mack," questioned why I wasn't with him in the RB but the commander gave him no specific reason. I was equally upset that I wasn't working with my regular group and hadn't been given any notice or reason. Later in the day, I confronted   Lt. "C" in his office and asked him why I was removed from the RB. He gave little more than a reiteration that I was looking "kind of tired." I expressed my outrage and demanded an acceptable explanation, but he would give me none. An hour or so later, I was called into Capt. "Gold's" office where he asked why I had complained to Lt. "C." After repeating my concerns to him, the captain gave me a half-hearted speech about how the administration wanted every officer to rotate assignments and become more familiar with the various post details. I knew this was a load of fertilizer. He pandered to me a bit by saying that I was "the best guy up there" but other officers were now going to take my place. I replied, "So, if I'm the best guy up there, does that mean you want the worst guy up there instead?" He assured me that replacement officers would be able to learn the routines, and I countered, "Yeah, but who's going to train them?" He ended the meeting by telling me that I wasn't going to work there any more, and that was final.

Interestingly, Capt. "Gold" began his career as a Correction Officer one month after I did, and we worked together several times on the old 4-12 shift. We were always friendly to each other; he once purchased a handgun and some scuba gear from me; but after we both moved to the 8-4 shift, he began a rapid sequence of promotions, culminating in the position of Deputy Superintendent, I believe. His friendliness and civility deteriorated as rapidly as he advanced.

Sadly, he was killed in an automobile accident a while later. Even though we were at odds professionally, I paid my respects by attending his funeral, writing and publishing a sympathetic, praise-filled article about him in a local newspaper. One of his family members called me while I was on the job to express appreciation for my tribute.

On my own time, I continued to investigate the reasons for my banishment from the RB and first discovered that several inmates who objected to my   enforcement of the rules and regulations wrote hateful, accusatory letters to   Lt. "C" and Correction Counselor "Anthony," the unit caseworker. There was nothing unusual about this, as inmates regularly complained and lied about treatment by officers. The stunning part was that this supervisor and counselor acknowledged the complaints without validating them, never once asking for my explanations. They were accepting the allegations of inmates against an officer, and rather than be pleased that I was doing such a good job, they decided that it was easier to move me out of the unit than to worry about what to do with the inmates. God forbid that convicts be inconvenienced by an officer who enforced the rules! "Anthony" had always been congenial towards me and regularly praised my efforts. He complimented me for helping him compile inmate updates by being able to quickly recall events like transfers and status changes without having to burrow through log books. He and Lt. "C" then went behind my back, took the inmate complaints to Capt. "Gold," and had me removed.

Three Tower

A Brief Flirtation With Promotion

By most accounts, I was considered to be a very competent and effective officer. My employee evaluations over the years were exemplary. One particular day in 1979, I was placed in charge of the third floor RB and was manning the control post when then-Lieutenant "Paul" arrived to conduct a routine inspection of the unit. During our conversation, he expressed his approval of my work ethic and suggested that I should apply for a promotion to the rank of sergeant. Being the sometimes-painfully honest man that I am, I thanked him for the encouragement but replied that I only had three years of experience at that time, was not yet familiar with all the particular posts and institutional job requirements, and didn't believe I was qualified for promotion at the time. The lieutenant appreciated my sincerity and understood my reasoning, but still recommended that I consider the option.

I witnessed many promotions during my tenure at Norfolk. A noticeable behavior among a few candidates was that regardless of their worthiness, they were willing to sacrifice principles and critical thinking for the sake of pleasing management in order to maintain their ranks. These officers, more often than not, developed unreasonable and unprofessional dispositions, exposing the errors of their advancements.

Sometime in the mid 1980s I felt confident and experienced enough to apply for promotion. A new facility, Old Colony Correctional Center in Bridgewater, Massachusetts, was preparing to open and job opportunities circulated throughout the DOC. I believed I could enjoy a new start as a sergeant there, had significant skills to offer, and lived closer to Old Colony than to Norfolk.

I passed the Civil Service promotional exam and was assigned an interview date at a central location inside the Bridgewater complex. My evaluators were a former Norfolk correction counselor and co-worker, a female manager with whom I was familiar, and an old, grizzled captain. They posed standard questions and then presented me with a problem to solve. The manager detailed a hypothetical scenario where I, as a sergeant, came upon two officers who were arguing about an order that the superintendent had issued and asked me how I would deal with them.

I said that I would explain the importance of following orders and instruct them to perform their duties accordingly. I hoped that the officers would respect me and my rank enough to comply. The captain then inquired as to what I would do if the officers blatantly refused the superintendent's order. Such behavior was highly unlikely, but I sensed where this interview was going. I stated that if they disobeyed *my* order, I would follow the chain of command and inform a superior officer of the situation for further action. My subconscious told me that the interviewers wanted me to say that I would "write those bastards up in a heartbeat!" In my experience, it was much more effective to solve a problem like this informally at first, pursuing discipline as a last resort. They didn't seem very satisfied with my answers, and I could feel the promotion slipping away. I would never sacrifice my principles, though.

The gruff captain then passed my latest attendance calendar across the table and asked if I noticed anything odd about it. It appeared fine to me. He told me to look at it again. I pointed out that I had only used three sick days and it was the best attendance year I had so far. He slid the form back to me again and said, "One more time!" It wasn't hard to read this guy's mind, so I responded, "Are you referring to the two sick days that were in conjunction with my days off?" The captain pulled back the paper and snarled, "Thank you!"

The panel dismissed me and said I'd receive a decision by mail. As I was leaving the building I spotted the new superintendent of Old Colony, a former fellow officer at Norfolk, having lunch in his office. I greeted him and he called me in to chat. He wished me luck on the promotion and said I'd make a good addition to the ranks at OCCC.

A short time later, I received the panel's decision by mail at Norfolk. The document contained categories for explaining their **_denial_** of my promotion. The first comment read "lack of training and experience." I had almost eight years on the job; scored well on the sergeant's exam and was recommended for promotion; completed refresher training courses; worked in cell blocks and open yards; completed transportation escorts; was qualified as an institutional disciplinary hearing officer; commissioned as a special state police officer; and had met all the requirements demanded of me. But in the confused minds of my interviewers, I didn't have enough "training and experience." The second notation was "interview," so obviously I didn't tell them what they wanted to hear. It seemed they preferred a sergeant who would follow rules to the letter;

would not think independently; would report every alleged misdeed to the administration; and help the superintendent mete out frequent discipline on line officers. The final check mark was made next to the word "other," and the written comment was "sick leave." God forbid that a sick day actually run in conjunction with a day off; that was not scientifically possible! I could thank the condescending captain for that jab. Come to find out, a number of officers with much less seniority and experience than I were promoted and transferred to Old Colony. This led me to the conclusion that the interviewers were weeding out promotional candidates that they considered might become "problematic" to management in Old Colony's future.

As aggravating as this denial was, it turned out to be a blessing in disguise. As OCCC progressed through its institutional infancy and I became more involved with the Massachusetts Correction Officers Federated Union, I was made aware that Old Colony's management was treating the rank and file very unfairly and unprofessionally. Supervisory harassment of officers was widespread. Reports were submitted describing the administration removing many chairs from within the facility to prevent officers from sitting down on the job. In particular, management removed a chair from an area of a softball field where officers would rest on occasion after making their rounds. The union was forced to file a complaint against the administration on the basis of what is termed the "right to sit law," and the chair was ultimately returned. Being a man of such intense principle and sensibility, I would have been quite unhappy working under such conditions.

I was wholeheartedly content to continue as a Correction Officer at Norfolk, and gave up any more thoughts of promotion. By the time I had completed ten years of service, I had enough seniority to earn a 7-3 shift position with Saturdays and Sundays off and could choose pretty much any vacation weeks I desired. Though attaining a higher rank would have increased my retirement pension, the immediate needs of my family were much more important. So, rather than having to return to a night shift as a new sergeant or lieutenant, with days off in the middle of the week, and be last on the list to choose vacation weeks, I settled for the status quo.

The Gatehouse

Transportation

Across the street from MCI Norfolk, a small wooden building served the dual purpose of providing employee training classrooms and the headquarters for a specialized group of officers assigned to the Central Transportation Unit (CTU), sometimes abbreviated as State Trans. Their responsibility was to escort inmates to court appearances, outside hospital appointments and transfers to and from correctional facilities. Those officers dressed in plain clothes instead of uniforms. Drivers of the cars and vans were armed, while unarmed officers maintained physical control of inmates that were secured in waist chains and leg irons.

A good many officers working inside the walls preferred the open environment of transportation details, and they regularly applied to fill vacant CTU positions. I, however, was not of the same mindset and preferred the controlled atmosphere of the segregation unit, tower duty or clerical work.

Occasionally, when State Transportation staff were all engaged or unavailable, shift commanders would assign uniformed officers to escort inmates to other destinations. I received my fair share of those details and many of them were quite unique and challenging.

The first that comes to mind involved driving an inmate to a specialty athletic shoe store to be fitted with medically prescribed footwear. Some bleeding-heart liberal judge had ordered this service in response to a frivolous lawsuit, so the taxpayers of Massachusetts were forced to finance the cost of the transportation plus $100 for high quality shoes given to some undeserving convicted felon. My partner and I expressed our disgust to fellow officers once we returned to the prison.

During one emergency ambulance transport, I was ordered to ride in the back of that vehicle beside an inmate who was terminally ill with Hepatitis, along with a medical technician. My shift commander insisted that I handcuff the inmate while he lay on the stretcher, but I chose not to do so. He was jaundiced and experiencing seizures, and was by no means an escape risk. I was more disturbed about sitting near someone who was infected with such a disease without being given some kind of protective covering. Fortunately, I never had to handle the inmate. We completed the mission without major problems, I never contracted the ailment, and the inmate died shortly after being admitted to an outside hospital. I guessed the shift commander was more concerned about some sick inmate escaping than the safety of his officer.

Sergeant "George" and I brought another inmate to an outside hospital for a series of medical tests that couldn't be performed at the prison. A nurse took a vial of blood, the inmate provided a urine specimen under our supervision, and then the nurse gave him a third vial and asked for a sperm sample. The sergeant and I were stunned and the convict was aghast when the nurse told him to go to the rest room to obtain the sample. Our mood soon changed to hilarity when the inmate asked for some pornography to help him with his efforts, but the nurse remained very sullen, especially after the inmate asked **her** to help him. We kept the inmate in leg irons but freed his hands from the waist chains. He retired to a toilet stall, but the embarrassment of the situation prevented him from providing the bodily fluid. He told the nurse that he was unable to comply with her request, so she asked if he could return the next day. He responded, "Lady, I'm in *prison!* I can't get out every day!" He even asked if he could obtain the sperm sample back in his housing unit, leave it on a kitchen warming table, and have it delivered to the hospital! The nurse coolly said the sample had to be fresh, and ultimately it was never obtained. We returned the inmate to the prison and tried to keep our chuckling to a minimum.

"George" and I teamed up again to transport a young, slightly built prisoner to a court appearance. This character was afflicted with a serious case of "little man's disease," acting as tough and intimidating as he could but not impressing anyone. His bark was definitely worse than his bite. He was serving a significant prison sentence but this particular court case was for some minor infraction. The judge and the attorneys conducted their business while the inmate's relatives watched the proceedings from the opposite side of the courtroom. Upon completion, the inmate, still in waist and leg restraints, attempted to walk over to where his family was sitting. I held him back and told him to move elsewhere. He shouted at me, "Fuck you, I don't do what you say!" I forced him to sit down and the sergeant told him to be quiet, but he yelled even louder, "Fuck you!" A court officer approached the inmate and instructed him to sit still and be quiet, but again he yelled, "Fuck you!" The judge finally banged his gavel and scolded the inmate, but he screamed back, "Fuck you, too!" The judge pounded the gavel again and shouted, "Thirty days in jail for contempt of court," and the convict hollered, "Fuck you," again! When the judge gave him thirty more days for contempt, the young man shouted, "I don't give a fuck, give me 100 years!" All the while, the inmate's family witnessed his antics and tearfully pleaded with him to behave. As we drove back to Norfolk, he actually asked Sgt. "George" and me, "You're not going to write me up, are you?" "Oh, no, of course not," we replied sarcastically. In addition to the extra sentence the judge handed him, the inmate received thirty days of isolation time in the RB and was reclassified to higher security based on my disciplinary report. Cursing at officers is one thing, but it certainly wasn't a wise idea for him to disrespect a judge.

The third time I teamed with Sgt. "George" to transport an inmate to court was one of the most unnerving details I experienced. The felon was implicated in a high profile case involving racial disturbances in the city of New Bedford, so extra security was deemed necessary. Sgt. "George" was the armed driver of our vehicle, while I sat in the back seat with the inmate to insure that he remained in restraints. A third officer followed us in another car, carrying a shotgun. When we arrived at the courthouse, we saw city police officers blocking off adjoining streets, armed court officers standing by as security escorts, and a large crowd of onlookers shouting support for the criminal. As if there wasn't enough disruption from the crowd, an old man started screaming racial epithets at the protestors from a second floor apartment window. Fortunately, no violence erupted. The only persons in the immediate congregation who weren't armed were the inmate and me, so I held him tightly as we entered the court and again when we returned to our vehicle. He was going to be my shield if I needed one.

I participated in a few more uneventful transportation details to outside hospitals and courtrooms during my career, but two of them stood out from the rest. My old 4-12 shift co-worker "Dominic;" Norfolk's version of "Mr. Congeniality," I would say facetiously; had spent many hours ingratiating himself with the various shift commanders in an attempt to obtain full time trip assignments, and this guy was a master of the art. He eventually was accepted into the CTU, trading his uniform for plain clothes.

When I checked the trip assignment board and saw that I was being forced to ride with "Dominic," another uniformed officer standing next to me wished me good luck and said, "Be sure to fasten your seat belt!" He had ridden with "Dominic" a day earlier. His advice was appreciated, but the cars back then had no seat belts. Our ride to Cambridge court was as hair-raising as a high speed chase. "Dominic" pushed the accelerator to the floor as often as he could, constantly blew the horn at other drivers and cursed his way to our destination. My heart was pounding as I recalled automobile accident analyses that showed front seat passengers usually suffered the greatest number of fatalities. The two inmates in the back seat were wearing security restraints but no seat belts, and they confided in me afterwards that they feared being slammed into the metal grill separating the front and back seats.

After we turned the inmates over to bailiffs, "Dominic" ignored me while playing poker with some court officers, killing time until the proceedings were through and we were to return to Norfolk. The only distraction in an otherwise boring, uneventful waiting period was seeing a former MCI Norfolk Correction Officer sitting in a holding cell, waiting for his court appearance. I was stunned to find him there and though he was no longer employed by the department, I remembered working with him on a few night shifts. We exchanged words briefly and he explained to me that he was being charged with narcotics offenses. I certainly couldn't offer him any sympathy. The ride back to Norfolk was another fast one but at least "Dominic" stayed off the horn for a change.

A week or so later, I was teamed with this gum-chewing, gruff-talking, wanna-be tough guy again, and with the experience of the last trip still fresh in my mind, I prepared myself as best I could. Once more, "Dominic" drove with the pedal to the metal, blue lights flashing and horn blaring. My knuckles were turning white from bracing myself against the dash board. He looked at me and said, "What's the matter, are you afraid?" I responded, "Yeah, I have a child about to be born and I'd like to live to see it!" He chuckled back, "Don't worry; I'm the world's greatest driver!" "Dominic" wore an easily recognizable but unattractive toupee, and the story behind it alleged that he was once in an auto accident and sustained a scalp injury, requiring an implanted hairpiece. This guy fancied himself a race car driver as well as a professional card dealer, but I was one of many co-workers who weren't impressed.

When we returned to Norfolk after that trip, I escorted the two frightened inmates to the prisoner entryway. "Dominic" dashed up the stairs and began removing their leg irons before they were secured in the holding area, demanding that the inmates be processed quickly because he wanted to collect his gear and leave early for a poker game. I entered the back room of the Gatehouse after the mission was completed and the shift commander asked me how the trip went. I immediately complained, "Never again!" When he asked what I meant by that, I explained my fear and the angst expressed by the inmates regarding my partner's reckless driving and told him that I would refuse to ride with this man again. The officer who gave me the initial advice to be careful when riding with "Dominic" was within earshot of the conversation and reported his apprehension to the shift commander as well. Not surprisingly, my comments found their way to the Transportation Unit and "Dominic" was reprimanded. He supposedly referred to me as "king rat" because I vocally objected to riding with him. If my complaints were at all responsible for his punishment and putting an end to my transportation assignments, I was eternally pleased.

Soon afterwards, I saw "Dominic" back in uniform, working inside the walls again. We rarely crossed paths during our respective assignments, but it didn't take long to learn the reason for his transfer.

As the story was told, "Dominic" was speeding excessively again during an inmate transportation and was stopped by a female Massachusetts State Police officer. He allegedly argued with the officer, flaunted the fact that he was driving an official vehicle, and then insulted her with the four-letter expletive that is considered most offensive to women. The trooper subsequently cited him for his reckless driving and when CTU managers were made aware of this, they chose to re-assign him for several weeks. Not surprisingly, "Dominic" managed to put his cozy social skills to good use again and somehow conned his way back into State Trans. Then, what does the Department of Correction do with an officer who has a bad attitude, a foul mouth, received a citation for speeding in a state vehicle, and was considered such a dangerous driver that other officers refused to ride with him? It promotes him to the rank of captain within the CTU! Is such an action nepotism or cronyism? Is it an innocent mistake, or is it just plain stupidity? Go figure!

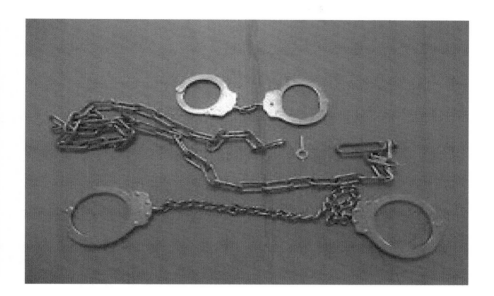

Attention Deficit

Correction Officers obviously have to maintain vigilance when monitoring inmates inside or outside of prison walls. Lapses of attention do happen, however, and they can lead to some very precarious situations.

In the late 1970s, the administration designated certain inmates as "trustees" and allowed them to work outside the walls. "Ralph," a well-known member of "organized crime" was mowing external lawn areas one morning without constant supervision. At some point during the day, the inmate could not be located. He had walked away, leaving the lawn mower behind, and was designated an escapee. A few other officers and I were armed, sent to monitor local road intersections and check vehicles passing by, but this inmate was long gone; no one thought otherwise.

Two officers were once assigned to secure a convict while he was a patient at an outside hospital. One carried a firearm while the other handled restraint equipment. As the story was told, the armed officer violated protocol by leaving the inmate's room while wearing the weapon, the unarmed officer failed to handcuff the patient to his bed, and the inmate suddenly sprang up and ran out of the building. He was ultimately apprehended by Boston Police officers, and the two Correction Officers were disciplined for their negligence. Not long afterwards, the armed officer was promoted to sergeant. Go figure, again....if you dare!

On another occasion, this same sergeant was in charge of the third floor RB. Some of the inmates confined there were violent troublemakers that had been transferred from MCI Walpole. Throughout the day, for some crazy reason, one frail young inmate named "Daniel" engaged in a verbal war with the Walpole bad-actors, enraging them and endangering himself. Some of those inmates were being let out of their cells one or two at a time to take showers. In another incredible lapse of judgment, the sergeant exited the secure control post and walked onto the tier, leaving the doors to the post and the cabinets containing the cell control switches open. One of the unescorted inmates finished his shower, then sneaked into the unguarded office, opened "Daniel's" cell door and those to some of his friends. A few of the Walpole convicts ran into their antagonist's cell and began beating him. The tier officers quickly restored order, the loud-mouthed inmate sustained a number of injuries, and the sergeant was demoted and disciplined along with some of the officers who were monitoring the activity.

For a time, Officer "Terry" was regularly assigned to the Administration Building Gate post, controlling ingress and egress to the prison yard through one gate and the Hospital through another. One day, he noticed an inmate janitor, who was cleaning the floor in that area of the building, simply stop his work and walk out the front door towards Five Tower, the Pedestrian Trap, and the prison exit. The officer claimed he panicked, tried to call for assistance, but never contacted anyone. The inmate was secured in the Five Tower Trap by the observant tower officer and Inner Perimeter Security officers responded to apprehend and lock up the felon.

The Ad Gate officer was soon called into the superintendent's office to explain what had happened. He asked for me to accompany him in my role of chief union steward. "Terry" admitted his foul-up, and the superintendent asked us what disciplinary sanction we thought would be appropriate for the mistake. I called for a letter of reprimand, but the boss insisted on something harsher.

I caucused privately with the officer and gave my opinion that he was going to receive at least a three-day suspension, which would have been difficult, if not impossible to successfully appeal. The union would have done so on his behalf, but the lengthiness of the proceedings would be indeterminate. His other option would be to willingly accept a one-day suspension and waive an appeal, which I believed would satisfy the superintendent. "Terry" chose that option, we presented it, and all parties agreed. He thanked me for my assistance and advice and was relieved to be receiving only one day without pay instead of three or more.

When a few union-haters heard of the arrangement, they criticized me for, in their simple minds, "selling him out," but Officer "Terry" set them all straight and stifled their whining by telling them that it was *his* choice to accept the sanction.

The Front Door

The "Uncivil" War

Massachusetts Correction Officers and support staff in departments like Maintenance and Prison Industries were initially represented by the umbrella union, American Federation of State, County and Municipal Employees (AFSCME), whose responsibility was to negotiate a collective bargaining agreement between Unit 4 employees and the state government, and represent union members at grievance and disciplinary hearings. In the late 1980s it became quite evident that the executives of this organization, along with local Norfolk union officials, were more interested in collecting dues than in fulfilling their obligations. Incidents of negligence, favoritism, theft, and intimidation by AFSCME supporters were witnessed but rarely reported for fear of retaliation.

The vending machines in the Gatehouse lobby were serviced by a select few officers known to have close ties with AFSCME and the local union leadership. When a significant amount of money from these machines was reported missing, a female State Police officer investigated the loss. Word filtered down that the detective knew who had stolen the money but couldn't prove it, so the case was closed. There was no doubt that those who filled the contents and withdrew cash from the vending machines were at fault, but no charges were filed. The theft faded into MCI Norfolk history nicknamed, "Quartergate!"

A short, spindly officer was assaulted and badly injured twice, simply because he was a supporter of a rival union that was in its formative stages. He was kicked in the abdomen by a much larger officer, an AFSCME "goon," but witnesses would not testify to the assault. A second time, he was slammed against a wall inside the Pedestrian Trap corridor, hit a mounted wooden box, and sustained a facial injury. This time, the assault was seen by many people. The victim had to be taken to a hospital for treatment, and the aggressor was disciplined.

Another officer told me he observed an AFSCME operative tampering with an unsecured ballot box, left unattended in the roll call room, but was afraid to complain about it. The outcome of that particular local election ran counter to all polling information, which indicated that the incumbent officials would lose to their challengers. This suggested that the malefactor had "stuffed" the ballot box to insure victory for AFSCME's "puppet regime."

In 1989, an upstart group of officers founded the Massachusetts Correction Officers Federated Union (MCOFU) and challenged AFSCME in a statewide election for representation of Unit 4 employees. At most of the correctional institutions, AFSCME "thugs" threatened and harassed supporters of the new union throughout the campaign, but when the votes were finally counted, MCOFU was the clear winner. The newly-formed independent had trounced an international umbrella union in its first contest. I came across AFSCME's former MCI Norfolk union president one day while he was griping and complaining about the election loss. In conversation, he asked for my opinion of the outcome and I told him point blank that if he and his group had conducted a "gentleman's campaign" instead of intimidating and assaulting employees, damaging vehicles, and destroying MCOFU signs, they would have won the election easily. He paused to think about that and then sadly agreed with me. I explained to him that a large number of voters went to the polls that day assuring AFSCME onlookers of their support, but when pen met paper, they chose exactly the opposite! It was not a surprise.

AFSCME leaders did not concede gracefully, though. They filed a challenge with the Massachusetts Labor Relations Commission, claiming that the election was flawed. The commission took the complaint under consideration, and the wait for its decision was marred by unforeseen circumstances.

We had been without a valid contract for some time and now we were forced to continue working under the provisions of an expired agreement, as negotiations between the MCOFU and the Commonwealth of Massachusetts were suspended pending the outcome of the challenge. AFSCME officials wasted no time in notifying Unit 4 employees that they were not required to associate with the MCOFU or pay union dues during this period. They solicited forms to those employees who had initially joined the MCOFU, telling them they could "sign out" while they waited for the final judgment. The new union depended on dues for its operation and had to suffice with contributions from a dwindling number of supportive members. Several of my friends had succumbed to the pressure and withdrawn their memberships, despite my encouraging them to stand strong and defend their rights. One co-worker, reportedly the final Norfolk officer to "sign out," was a military combat veteran. I was astonished to see such a solid MCOFU supporter succumb to that kind of pressure. He told me the AFSCME "dopes" had been "busting his balls" constantly so he left the MCOFU just to make them stop.

I was never the biggest, baddest, toughest guy on the block, but I was one of a very few officers who had the intestinal fortitude to stand up to the AFSCME bullies. I could outthink them with half my brain tied behind my back, and I made it well known that if anyone ever assaulted me or damaged my vehicle because of my union affiliation, I would prosecute them to the fullest extent of the law. I had no fear of being called a "rat" for testifying against a co-worker's wrongdoing and my principles were indelible. AFSCME advocates had no problem being sarcastic and condescending to me, but I was never assaulted nor was my car vandalized. It only took a little bit of political courage and willpower to keep them at bay, something a good many officers apparently didn't possess.

While the election challenge plodded along, AFSCME "roughnecks" demanded that MCOFU officials debate them in a public forum. There was no need for such a confrontation, but that didn't stop AFSCME's persistence. They publicized a time and place for the meeting, rented a local VFW hall, and stocked it with partisans who planned to shout down any MCOFU points of view. Rather than step into such a precarious situation, MCOFU Executive Board members hired a professional clown and sent him to the gathering in their stead.

He presented the AFSCME officials with a booklet entitled "AFSCME CONTRACT," the pages of which were all blank. The written message he delivered said, "Sending a clown to debate clowns!" The poor guy had to flee the hall, fearing for his life when the crowd erupted. This response by the MCOFU board members was a stroke of genius, and the sight of AFSCME "dopes" coming unhinged in the Norfolk roll call room the next day was priceless.

For several months, AFSCME propagandists pushed the mantra, "There's going to be a new election in two weeks!" Those time frames kept passing without results. Finally, the Labor Commission issued a several page report, with the summary stating, in essence, "There will be *no* new election!" The appeal was dismissed and the MCOFU was finally certified. Being a union steward, I received a copy of the decision and showed it to one of the intellectually- challenged officers who kept insisting there would be a new election. I handed him the document; written on the commission's letterhead; signed by three commissioners. He read it, gave it back to me and said, "That's a bunch of bullshit; you made that up!" My immediate response was, "Somebody ought to shoot you with a nice silver bullet and put you out of your misery!" What else can be said to an ideologue that completely dismisses a proven fact?

The former members who had initially "signed out" rejoined the union, but MCOFU officials now had the legal authority to deny membership to certain employees because of their obstructionist and uncivil behavior towards the new union and its supporters. There were seven such individuals at MCI Norfolk. Two of them actually begged my forgiveness for the way they treated me, but it took me quite some time to accept their apologies. Another one came to me and said that he and the rest of the ostracized officers would gladly join the MCOFU if we simply replaced the union president. My retort was that I'd much rather keep the union president and get rid of all the AFSCME "dopes."

An order was then passed down from the Department of Correction requiring every Unit 4 employee to join the union or sign agency service fee agreements within 30 days or be terminated, as some kind of membership was mandatory. The AFSCME characters began scampering to MCOFU stewards and the Norfolk Treasurer's Office looking for forms to sign to prevent losing their jobs. It was delicious to see union thugs and bullies in distress after all the grief they had given the rest of us. The seven excluded officers were allowed entry into the MCOFU as agency fee payers only. They would be entitled to all the merits of the collective bargaining agreement but none of the union benefits. They certainly didn't deserve any forgiveness.

Many of the AFSCME troublemakers continued to criticize the MCOFU's efforts to improve wages, benefits and working conditions for Unit 4 employees, similar to the way congressional Democrats so frequently villainize Republicans who create legislation that would better the lives of Americans. More times than I care to remember I was forced to expose AFSCME lies and dress down whining fellow officers. The former local AFSCME vice-president even threatened to kill me if I tampered with the bid system, wrongly believing I was going to do so. I stood my ground against this bloviator and he backed down. To the contrary, I never intended to, nor did I ever impede that system, and received no complaints when I worked in the Assignment Office. The one benefit that arose from this veiled threat was that the perpetrator never spoke to me again.

In the face of never-ending AFSCME hate-filled rhetoric, the initial collective bargaining agreement between our MCOFU and the Commonwealth was the first state contract in Massachusetts history that was **unanimously** approved by the legislature. Employees received retroactive pay raises, enhanced benefits, clearer language, and upgraded working conditions. Even though this agreement was an enormous improvement over previous contracts, some MCOFU-haters still complained about it. I overheard one officer griping about his union dues being raised fifty cents a week, while looking at a paycheck that included a fifteen percent increase in pay! One of my fellow union stewards gave this guy quite a verbal beating for his foolishness.

Even though this agreement was now law, it didn't stop the Department of Correction and local institution managements from violating it. More than once, a captain or deputy said to me, "This is YOUR contract, not mine," forcing me to show him the official signatures and reminding him that it was EVERYONE'S contract!

The Disciplinary Office

In the late 1980s I was trained to conduct inmate disciplinary hearings. With my affinity for language and creative writing, I found the job easy to understand and perform. Inmates are responsible for adhering to institutional and departmental rules and regulations, and the list of infractions they must avoid is presented to them upon their incarceration. If a correctional employee wrote a disciplinary report, called a "ticket," alleging an inmate violated one or more rules, the Disciplinary Officer; usually a lieutenant, sometimes a sergeant, appointed by the superintendent; would process the report and assign another officer to conduct an administrative hearing. It is not a court of law, and judicial protocol is not adopted. A three-member panel consisting of the hearing officer, another security employee, and a correction counselor would interview the subject of the report, consider witness testimony and physical evidence, and listen to the reporting staff person's explanation. After deliberating, the panel would agree on a sanction, give the inmate a copy of the result, and the inmate was then allowed to appeal the decision to the superintendent if he wished.

I chaired scores of hearings during my time in the Disciplinary Office, even a few at MCI Walpole, but a particular one at Norfolk was a real highlight. Inmate

"Peter," one of the most notorious convicts in Massachusetts DOC history, spent most of his incarceration in segregation and received hundreds of disciplinary reports for assaults, contraband, threats and the like. Inmates were allowed to have actual attorneys represent them despite the hearings not being courts of law, and on this day two lawyers, one male and one female, advocated for inmate "Peter." I made sure to audiotape the proceedings to have a record of the conversations. The male attorney was civil and somewhat respectful. The inmate was loud and boisterous, as was his character, and denied any wrongdoing. However, the woman lawyer was nasty, condescending, and out of line to the point where I was forced to call for a female officer to escort her out of the prison. The reporting officer then gave his testimony, and I concluded the hearing. It was mind-boggling to all of us that such lawyers would actually waste time trying to defend this inmate, whose disciplinary history created the largest file on record.

Towards the end of my service in the D-Office, there was a sudden influx of disciplinary reports being submitted by officers from the Inner Perimeter Security team. They had been conducting wide surveillance of inmates in particular areas of the prison and were apprehending many of them for drug-related activities. All of the hearings that I and other officers conducted produced guilty findings based on testimonies and evidence presented. However, we were unaware that the inmates were submitting appeals to new Superintendent "Arthur" and he, in turn, was blindly granting these appeals and dismissing the tickets. The IPS officers who worked so hard to discover inmate drug violations were outraged and several of them voiced their complaints to the Disciplinary Office. We hearing officers were definitely sympathetic, as we had found all these inmates guilty, and we urged our supervisor, Lieutenant "Gib," to express everyone's displeasure to the superintendent. "Gib" claimed he spoke with "Arthur" about these problems, but he was never forceful or supportive of the cause and failed to defend the IPS and his hearing officers.

At some point during this fiasco, Lt. "Gib" was replaced by a new Disciplinary Officer, Lt. "Brian." "Gib" took some extended time off and then faded into obscurity. "Brian" was much more concerned for his fellow officers and voiced his objections to so many D-report guilty findings continuing to be overturned by "Arthur." The ultimate insult to prison security came when the superintendent released inmate "Peter" from segregation, placed him into the general population, and gave him a job in the metal shop of the Industries Building. What a brilliant move; allowing one of the most assaultive inmates access to pieces of sharpened metal with which to create "shanks;" homemade knives!

Superintendent "Arthur" and Deputy "Gold" then had me removed from the Disciplinary Office. I imagined they weren't fond of my union activities in addition to my hearing decisions. I wrote several incident reports to both the Norfolk administration and to the MCOFU Executive Board concerning the absurd security problems the superintendent was creating. Fortunately, union officials raised a collective ire with the correction commissioner's office and publicized their complaints in the media. The commissioner acknowledged this dysfunctional situation and made some significant changes. He ordered all the D-report appeals that were granted by "Arthur" to be reviewed. He also directed that inmate "Peter" be removed from general population and the metal shop, returned to segregation, and eventually transferred back to MCI Walpole. The commissioner then replaced "Arthur" with a new superintendent, reassigning him elsewhere within the department. I was significantly proud of the fact that my efforts to maintain the integrity of the Disciplinary Office and the safety of my fellow officers resulted in the lockup of a problematic inmate and the removal of a totally incompetent superintendent. It was an example of how impactful a combination of courageous officers and an effective union leadership could be.

The MCOFU president called to tell me of "Arthur's" reassignment and that inmate "Peter" was removed from the prison population, kicking and screaming. The following day, while assigned to the Ad Building Gate post, I was relating the story to Lt. "B" when the superintendent hustled past us on the way to his office. Lt. "B" said to him, "Sorry to hear about you leaving," and "Arthur" shouted back, "No you're not....no you're not....you had something to do with this, too!" Lt. "B" actually had no involvement with this change, but I enjoyed immensely seeing "Arthur" come unglued in such a manner. It was a fitting end to a superintendent who coddled convicts, was disrespectful to many employees, and had no business being promoted to such a position in the first place.

Massachusetts Department of Correction

MCI Norfolk

Contraband discovered by Special Operation Division

- Sharpened flat stock discovered in front of Unit 1-1

 Massachusetts Department of Correction

Adversarial Administrations

One fact of life in the Correction Officer business that many of us learned very quickly was that prison managers, in general, were **not** our friends; they were our employers. When I began in 1976, Acting Superintendent "Ted" was in charge of MCI Norfolk. He was promoted through the ranks and came across as a stern man, scornful of officers who utilized their earned sick leave. I confess that I did take my one and only illegitimate sick day in August 1976 because I had a hot date that night, then I used one legitimate sick day in October, another in November, and a third in December; one day a month for three consecutive months. "Ted" called me to his office, along with my shift commander, ADS "Arnold," to chastise me for using the sick days and tell me that I would have to submit medical evidence for any absence during the next six months. Then, my attendance calendar would be reevaluated. Without an argument, I merely replied, "No problem," and started to leave his office. "Arnold" then barked, "You know why he said 'no problem?' His father is his family doctor!" I wish I had a photograph of their expressions, just for posterity! I did make them pointedly aware that my father was an ethical man and would not provide fraudulent medical evidence to **anyone**, including me!

Since I used no sick days for the following half-year, I was taken off the "doctor'snote" requirement. It bears noting that "Ted" allegedly used up all or most of **his** sick leave, legitimate or otherwise, before retiring.

The first appointed superintendent I worked for was "Michael." He was an experienced manager who came from outside the Massachusetts system. My initial encounter with him was in the fall of 1977 when he visited the 4-12 shift during a dinner break at the OIC. He seemed very congenial and supportive of the officers. The only other time I had any conversation with him was during the infamous Blizzard of '78, when he allowed me to go home to rest as long as I returned to work my required sixteen hours.

When I first joined the 8-4 shift, "Bill" was another officer who advanced through the ranks to become superintendent. The best that could be said about this character was that he usually appeared to be oblivious to the reality of the day. He fancied himself an intellectual but didn't appear very genuine. One day, back when he held the rank of supervisor, he was conducting a classroom instruction. He wrote an assortment of Massachusetts General Laws and their ID numbers on a blackboard and was explaining them as if they pertained to the Department of Correction. Officer "Dapper" was in attendance and said he recognized some of the language as being real estate law. He brought that to the attention of the class, and "Bill's" embarrassment quickly became obvious. As superintendent, "Bill's" most notable policy change was moving shift start times forward one hour.

Our next superintendent was also an officer who had risen through the ranks, almost exclusively on the 12-8 shift. "Norm" was arguably the most contemptible person I ever worked with, beginning with his behavior as a Midnight Shift supervisor during the Blizzard of '78. His legacy was one of bitterness and scorn for line officers, plus harsh and unfair discipline. A local AFSCME official once described to a group of officers the assortment of perks the union was going to extract from "Norm" at a labor-management meeting, but afterwards the rep complained that the only item the superintendent conceded was allowing officers to wear baseball-style caps instead of the old, hard-brimmed hats. "Norm" was also witnessed to be a sexual predator of sorts, regularly trying to lavish his attention on female employees. The women officers that I knew were approached by "Norm" all forcefully rejected his advances, but he was observed many times carousing with one particular female civilian office worker. Another report claimed he once ordered some officers out of the Gatehouse basement exercise area so he and his female companion could work out and shower afterwards.

Superintendent "V" eventually replaced "Norm" and was similarly unreasonable towards Correction Officers. His was a non-security frame of reference. Managers who came from what we called the "social-worker ranks" often carried themselves as intellectually superior to officers. "V" was frequently at odds with the Massachusetts Correction Officers Federated Union with regard to employee discipline and tenets of the collective bargaining agreement. This made for a very hostile work environment. He was later appointed DOC commissioner. Where else would a problematic administrator go but *up* the crony career ladder?

We then had to endure the short-lived regime of Superintendent "Arthur" who, as I mentioned earlier, gave favored treatment to inmates at the expense of officers.

"Arthur" was replaced by Superintendent "Pete," also from the social worker ranks, but he proved to be infinitely more reasonable than most of his predecessors. I was Norfolk's chief union steward during his administration and we had a good working relationship. At times he would utter the worn-out phrase, "We agree to disagree," but he showed respect for officers and the union for the most part and was given the appropriate respect in return. His deputy superintendent and director of security were former Correction Officers, equally fair-minded. For the most part, "Pete" treated our collective bargaining agreement seriously and took steps to improve working conditions within the prison.

The DOC developed a procedure of rotating superintendents throughout the system every year or so, still apparently more concerned about "stagnation" than performance. In my last year before retirement, Superintendent "D" managed MCI Norfolk. His reputation from a previous assignment was marred by an uncooperative relationship with officers and the union. He continued this posture at Norfolk, somewhat reminiscent of Supt. "Arthur." Supt. "D" carried on the practice of what was called "happy hour," where the superintendent and selected staff presented themselves to the inmate population on the Quad at regular times in order to address grievances and complaints. Security staff considered these events to be foolish, risky, and another example of coddling convicts. A couple of years after I retired, I read a media story of how Supt. "D"had been stabbed by an inmate at one of the "happy hour" gatherings. It was just another inevitability.

The Quad

Employee Relations

Basic human nature dictates that employees in any business will be subjected to positive and negative interactions at some point in their careers. The Department of Correction is no exception, although it should be. Correction Officers work in a dangerous environment and their instincts for camaraderie and concern for the safety of co-workers are similar to those developed by military service people, law enforcement agencies, and firefighters. However, personalities are what they are, and people are imperfect. The most important traits I expected to find in fellow employees were fairness and reasonableness, but such was not always the case.

I had to rely on veteran officers to provide real on-the-job training and I planned on doing the same for new employees once I gained experience. As mentioned earlier, two months after I started, I saw new officer "Dominic" sitting alone on a lobby bench before the 4-12 shift roll call. I greeted him in a friendly manner as I walked past him, but he only returned a scowl. A few weeks passed, I would still speak to him but he never acknowledged me. We hadn't worked together yet since we were both being teamed with more seasoned officers.

Unfortunately, it was only a matter of time before we were paired, assigned to the "Sevens" one night, where our duties kept us in different areas until we were to start counting the Seven Block units at 10pm. At that hour, we met up with a 10-6 officer to complete the three-man counting crew, and I merely asked if they wanted to base in one particular unit. "Dominic" insisted we had to start in another unit, and when I asked what the difference was, he shouted at me, "*Listen*, you, I've been here two months and I get the 'Sevens' every Monday and this is the way it's done!" Our base unit was irrelevant, but I went along with his choice without arguing. I could see how hostile this character was going to be as our careers pressed on, and I definitely wanted no more part of him.

A while later, I was assigned to Three Tower for the 4-12 shift. It was possible to connect all the tower phones through the Gatehouse telephone system so officers could stay in contact with each other, relay information, and remain awake. This particular night we were discussing seniority and one of the other officers asked me if I knew the start dates of a few co-workers. "Dominic's" name only came up to identify his seniority position but somehow, someone told him that he had been mentioned during the tower talk. He came up to me a couple of nights later and said, "Hey, *you*, I want to talk to you!" He started barking, "I know you were talking about me...," but I stopped him in his tracks to say that the subject of our talk was simply seniority. He then started, "I know you hate my guts...," to which I interrupted that I didn't hate his guts nor did I know where he got that idea from. He seemed to calm down, so I explained to him that there were several ways to approach people, all of which could exact different responses. For example, one officer could courteously remind another to turn on a specific outdoor light, or he could growl, "Hey, you, turn that light on!" "Dominic" usually came across with the latter tone. I also suggested that he stop feeling paranoid, because no one was "talking about him." I did my best to be civil to this guy but didn't receive much civility in return.

For a brief time in the 1980s, the Department of Correction analyzed officers' job performances in consideration of awarding "merit raises." That appeared to be an appropriate benefit and an incentive for officers to step up their efforts to obtain the best possible evaluations. If I remember correctly, I received the bonus. However, there were two particular officers who worked in the exact same area, had relatively the same amount of seniority, and were given identical reviews, but only one received the payment. Management gave no explanation for this decision, and there was no way to assuage the anger of any officer who was slighted. It created unwarranted animosity between officers and generated more disgust towards the administration.

A general understanding was that the top three sources of problems encountered by Correction Officers were, in order, management; our own co-workers; and then the convicts. This was definitely a sad state of affairs. During my career, I tried to create a working relationship with inmates. I enforced institutional rules, wrote multiple disciplinary and incident reports, but never mistreated a convict. Based on the number of complaints by RB inmates submitted to caseworkers and the unit manager, I was one of the most despised officers in the segregation area, simply because I was doing my job. Those reactions were expected from inmates. Fortunately, I was only assaulted four times in twenty years, all happening in the RB, but was never injured.

What I never saw coming was the conspiracy by an RB correction counselor, the unit lieutenant and a captain to remove me from the building and assign me

elsewhere. Even though the captain said I was "the best guy for the job" in the RB, it was easier to move me than to transfer inmates, and a naïve' management apparently believed that the inmates would behave much better if I wasn't supervising them. I also was disturbed by the RB lieutenant's disrespect towards me. We were carpool partners at one time, but after he became a member of the IPS team, he started driving alone, becoming very scornful and overbearing as he continued to rise through the ranks.

Even though lieutenants were members of the Correction Officers union and were considered "labor" as opposed to "management," some of them were given administrative assignments. Lt. "B" was once ordered to review officers' attendance calendars, something that was actually the responsibility of a captain or other manager. He interviewed me once and criticized my absences, asking, "How can we help you with your sick leave?" I replied, "Just get off my back and leave me alone! It's no one's business how I utilize my sick leave!" He then said, "Oh, by the way, we don't necessarily have to accept your father's doctor's notes," even though he was my family physician. He was insinuating that my dad's medical evidence explaining my absences could be fraudulent. I hollered back at Lt. "B," "You damned well **better** accept my father's notes or you'll be receiving phone calls you're not going to like!" Needless to say, my medical evidence was never rejected and the practice of lieutenants reviewing sick leave was eventually discontinued.

At my father's wake in 1989, I shared a sobering moment regarding authorized leave with Capt. "Rich" and Lt. "B," who were kind enough to pay their respects, and my mother. She was fully aware of how DOC management sometimes mistreated employees because of their absences. After I introduced her to my two superior officers, she stated to them, "Oh, I'm so glad you came because now you can confirm that when Joe said his father died, he wasn't lying!" Capt. "Rich" and Lt. "B" were dumbfounded and tongue-tied, but it was clear by their expressions that they received the message!

The most infuriating incident of management abuse I ever encountered occurred in February 1981 when I was on the 10-6 shift. The administration issued every employee some kind of medical information form to be filled out by their primary care physicians and returned to the Treasurer's Office by a certain deadline. My father was still my family doctor, but he was out of state at the time. I was a single parent and my family needs restricted me to working only the 10pm to

6am shift hours. Since I would be unable to return the medical form by the deadline, I sent a letter to the Treasurer explaining that I would comply with the request as soon as my father returned. I was not about to waste time and resources seeking out another physician for such a minor request. On the next payday, I went to receive my check but the Gatehouse officer dispensing them told me it was missing. There was definitely subterfuge in the works. My personal schedule required me to return home after my shift, take my young son to a babysitter, sleep till 2pm, then bring my son home. He and I were living with my elderly aunt then, but she was unable to care for him during waking hours.

I needed my paycheck, so in place of precious sleep time, I had to travel back to Norfolk to find out why I hadn't been paid. Even though I was still in uniform and told the Gatehouse sergeant that I needed to go to the Treasurer's Office, he wouldn't allow me to enter. I sensed that someone knew why I was returning to the prison, and my stunned reaction, frustration and anger were coalescing quickly. Suddenly, the local AFSCME president and vice president arrived and instead of representing and defending me, as was their obligation, they escorted me into the Deputy Superintendent's office as if I was an inmate. To my surprise, the deputy was my former 4-12 shift commander, "Arnold." He snarled at me for failing to submit the medical form in the required time; for having the audacity to write what he called a "nasty" letter to the Treasurer's Office; and creating such a "hostile" situation! He added, "You also said something about we're not fucking with a rookie because you have five years in - well, we don't consider guys to be veterans until they have **six** years in!" **What?** (If I had written "six years," he would have said, "seven!")

I refused to back down from the deputy, repeated the content of my letter, which was by no means "nasty," and said I was not refusing to submit the form, simply waiting for my family doctor to return. I also reminded him that it was illegal to withhold an employee's paycheck without just cause, adding, "If I didn't need the damned check right now I'd have an attorney call and you could explain to **him** why you're holding it!" That comment changed the tone of our conversation. He then handed me the paycheck along with a blank medical form and asked me if I'd consent to have the prison doctor fill it out. In the interest of harmony and ending this fiasco, I agreed. The prison doctor only took my blood pressure, then signed the form; so much for "important information" being needed! The worthless union reps who followed me through the ordeal actually

insisted that I go to the Treasurer's Office and apologize to the lady who received my letter. **I** was the one who was wronged here, but these clowns wanted **me** to apologize? In order to retain my dignity and to give a bit of a slap to the union officials, I went to the Treasurer's Office and approached the noticeably anxious clerk. She reacted as if I was going to become violent, which was definitely not the case. I told her that I would apologize for the situation getting so out of hand, but I would never apologize for **my** actions! She understood and we were both quite relieved. I then expressed my displeasure to the useless AFSCME reps and went home.

For a time when I was on the 10-6 shift, I used to count the Four Block units on Wednesdays with the same two 4-12 officers, "Steven" and "Robert." Between the 10pm and 11pm counts, we had roughly forty minutes of down time, so we played cards in our base unit office. We were awake and attentive, but management frowned upon card playing or reading on duty. Sleeping on the job was obviously a terminable offense. "Steven" and I remained Correction Officers and friends for our careers, but "Robert" made his way up the promotional ladder. As he reached lieutenant and then captain, he became less agreeable and more abrasive and imperious towards officers with whom he formerly worked. When I once reminded him of how he used to play cards and read while on duty in years earlier, he flat out denied ever doing so.

"Don L" was another officer who was hastily promoted to sergeant, lieutenant and captain. Like Capt. "Robert," he was abusive, incompetent, and disrespectful to line officers. While I was working in the Assignment Office one day, Capt. "Don L" asked me to complete some paperwork for him. No sooner had I begun the chore, he reassigned me to assist in processing inmates for transportation. The shift was short-handed, as was often the case, and I had insufficient time to finalize all my clerical requirements. As I was delivering daily rosters to the Gatehouse control room, I crossed paths with Capt. "Don L" who asked me if I had finished his project. When I reminded him that I had been reassigned for a while and didn't have time to complete his request, he yelled at me,

"Well, if you did your *fucking* job!" **He** was the cause of my being time constrained, and then he accused *me* of not doing my job? I erupted back at him, undeterred by his rank, and started walking towards him. Inside the control room, Sgt. "Kenny" and Officer "Karen" witnessed the interchange. "Karen" tapped on the window glass to get my attention and whispered to me, "Don't do

it; it's not worth it!" Fortunately, I took her advice and walked away from the argument instead of escalating it.

I was not about to sit back and submit to such managerial abuse, so I filed a union grievance against Capt. "Don L." Generally, these complaints slowly make their way from review by the superintendent, to a Step 2 hearing with a representative from the correction commissioner's office, to a Step 3 appeal at the Office of Employee Relations (OER). Beyond those hearings, the union retained the option to force the issue to binding arbitration, the Mass. Civil Service Commission or the Mass. Labor Relations Commission. This progression through appellate forums was a sinful waste of time, money and energy, but the leadership of the MCOFU made every effort to support its members and uphold the collective bargaining agreement. Being the chief union steward at Norfolk added a special emphasis to my grievance.

On the day of my Step 3 hearing, the Norfolk superintendent was forced to grant release time to Capt. "Don L" and Personnel Director "Dick" to answer my charges, along with witnesses Sgt. "Kenny" and Officer "Karen" who traveled with me to OER in Boston. Losing three line officers for this period of time left the shift even more short-handed. The MCOFU

Grievance Coordinator and union attorney met us there. It's fair to say that none of us wanted to suffer through such an unnecessary and time-consuming event, but principle was at stake here. After reviewing the facts of the case and the details of my report, the OER hearing officer met privately with the representatives of management and the union and constructed a settlement agreement which would hopefully satisfy both sides. A settlement is generally not considered an admission of guilt, though it insinuates as much. My greatest desire was to see Capt. "Don L" disciplined for his behavior, but such was not included in the consensus. Management agreed to refrain from future animosity as was displayed by Capt. "Don L," to maintain staffing in the Assignment Office for the full 7-3 shift, and an assortment of stipulations which could be used by the union as precedents in future disputes. To my displeasure, I was encouraged by my supporters to accept the agreement because it was preferable to win a partial victory than to gamble and perhaps lose the entire case later on.

The Assignment Office

One of the more unique positions on the Day Shift was that of Assignment Officer. The duties were clerical in nature and included drafting the rosters which Day Shift commanders used to distribute appropriate security staffing. These forms contained names of officers scheduled for duty and those who were on approved leave.

The Assignment Officer was also responsible for maintaining the annual vacation board and addressing occasional time card concerns, but the most critical function affecting every officer was to preserve the integrity of the shift and days off bid system.

At the discretion of the superintendent or his designee, officer positions that became vacant through retirement, transfer, promotion, resignation, or termination would be listed on a common bulletin board as open and available. Officers submitted bid slips requesting to be awarded these shifts and days off based on their seniority, and the Assignment Officer was charged with accurately verifying time in service. During my first few years, one seasoned veteran officer occupied this position.

He was a well-known character, but his eccentricities were sometimes the stuff of legend. He could be jovial and friendly or sarcastic and miserable, depending on the situation. It was a widely held belief that he would occasionally pilfer another officer's lunch on a whim, with little remorse. A story circulated that one particular day, an officer who had previously been victimized by this man prepared a surprise meal for him containing a powerful laxative. On schedule, he stole the food, consumed it and had to endure the aftereffects for the remainder of the day. This incident allegedly cured him of his food theft habit, but that remained unconfirmed.

Behavior like this could be tolerated to a certain degree, but tampering with the job bid system was totally unacceptable. Since there are "no secrets in the big house," a number of officers became aware of some unforced errors in the awarding of bids. Rumors began surfacing that this Assignment Officer could be bribed with submarine sandwiches in exchange for some kind of favoritism.

Although I know of no direct evidence to substantiate this claim, I, myself, was a victim of an inappropriately awarded bid. I had submitted a request for a 7-3 shift position with Wednesdays and Thursdays off, but that spot was given to an officer with less seniority. I voiced my objection to the Assignment Officer and instead of immediately rectifying the error, he responded by saying, "Don't worry, I'll *give* you Wednesdays and Thursdays off." He had no authority to randomly assign days off, but whatever his actions were, I ultimately received the bid that I had won. To me, the most disturbing part of this controversy was that the Assignment Officer appeared to be making job bid decisions on his own, without a captain's approval. Shift and days off placements are very personal issues to Correction Officers and the respect for seniority was always of primary importance. Seniority was the one thing that no one could take away from us.

Sometime in 1992, MCOFU Executive Board members and MCI Norfolk management discussed reports of corruption within the Assignment Office and reached an agreement to have 7-3 shift commanders place a union steward as a second officer in that post. The seasoned veteran had moved on, and I was selected to begin training with his replacement, experienced Assignment Officer "Karen." Though I had never worked with her before, "Karen" and I had always been friendly towards one another. However, our new working relationship had been tainted by false information given her by Capt. "Don L."

As I discussed this new two-person working condition with "Karen," I discovered that the captain led her to believe that I was replacing her permanently and that the union was responsible for kicking her out. I assured her that this was patently false and appeared to be a deliberate ploy by Capt.

"Don L" to put her at odds with the union and with me personally. Fortunately, we broke the ice without animosity, became great friends, and she trained me very well in the Assignment Office duties, to the point where I could handle the responsibilities alone if necessary.

Over time, the rank and file exhibited considerably greater faith and trust in the efficiency of the Assignment Office. C.O. "Karen" remained number one in that post and I was her trusty sidekick for quite some time. Two other officers who had also received appropriate training filled in when neither of us was on duty. The Assignment Office was running like a well-oiled machine and complaints by officers to the union were few and far between. But, as life in general dictates, good things usually come to an end. The Day Shift continued experiencing staffing shortages and shift commanders were forced to pull officers from certain posts and reassign them where they were most needed. The second person in the Assignment Office was a luxury that could be done without, and was often utilized to assist with duties such as inmate transportation preparations. The Assignment Office duties could be completed by one experienced officer, but that required considerably more time, which affected both quality and quantity. Delays in the posting of open bids became sources of frustration for line officers.

On one particular day, without warning, I was placed in the Assignment Office, but Officer "Karen" was re-assigned to the Gatehouse outer control. This was confusing to us, since she was the senior officer in that post and it was expected that I would have been the one sent elsewhere. There existed an ingrained feeling in most, if not all officers that receiving an unexpected job change was some form of discipline or mistreatment, and "Karen" and I shared that angst.

Remembering back to my early days at the institution, it was standard practice to have officers gain experience through rotational assignments, and then after a number of years settle into a regular post; perhaps a desk job, in a tower, or some other preferred location. That perception changed drastically in the mid to late 1980s when management developed a mindset that stagnation was the result of an officer remaining in a certain post for a long time, regardless of whether he or she was proficient and effective. Shift commanders were insisting that every officer should learn all the functions of the institution through constant job changes. This was a hard sell, though, because most of us knew this practice was used to keep officers off balance, making them easier to control.

View of West Field from Two Tower

Retaliation

As time progressed, I found myself working solo in the
Assignment Office while Officer "Karen" was regularly in the
Gatehouse. I had won my grievance against Capt. "Don L"
and came away with binding orders that could be beneficial to
other officers within the department, but I never received the
remedy I desired; discipline for "Don L."

My final reward was being replaced and ousted from the Assignment Office, never to return. Capt. "Don L" made me part of the regular officer rotation in the Departmental Segregation Unit (DSU), first floor RB. I was back in my favorite building but was stuck in a "program" rather than simply dealing with locked-up inmates. However, after a short time, I regained my sense of purpose and blended in well with a new group of officers.

There were now fewer Walpole 10-Block trouble-making inmates confined there and more cooperative convicts who had at least some desire to complete the "program" and return to general population or be released. That's not to say there was never a problem on that floor.

A black inmate had been confined to his cell for disciplinary reasons and was creating quite a commotion. The 7-3 shift commander was in the DSU office conducting a routine inspection, heard the noise, and ordered me to bring the inmate to him. Though it was not necessarily a wise procedure, it was customary to allow an inmate to leave the tier unrestrained, and I escorted this complainant to speak with Capt. "James." He aired his gripes, sought sympathy and resolution, but the captain was having none of it. He ordered the inmate to return to his cell, but as I walked him back, the convict suddenly stopped and refused to move. I ordered him several times to keep walking, but he stood still. When I attempted to place him in handcuffs, he resisted, and as quickly as Officer "Marc" responded to my altercation with inmate "Renaldo" years earlier, three officers quickly arrived to help me take the inmate to the floor, handcuff him, and carry him back to his cell.

Not long after this incident I was on duty for a disturbance that turned out to be as comical as it was dangerous. The DSU inmates were eating breakfast in the locked dining area. A young white inmate, who worked as a houseman, was serving fried eggs when a younger black inmate began having words with him. The two had been at odds with each other a day earlier but had kept their distance. Sgt. "Bob" was in the unit office, C.O. "Jeff" was manning Post One, controlling the sally port that allowed access to the DSU tier; the office and dining room; the outside yard and the floors above; and the exit from the RB into the Ad Building. I was on the closed tier conducting cell searches, and our fourth officer was on an errand outside the building. Without warning, we heard the crash of falling plastic dishes and metal pans coming from the dining room. A fight had broken out between the houseman and the black inmate. I hollered to Officer "Jeff" to let me out of the tier so I could respond, but he was on the telephone trying to call the institution emergency number. Later on, we found out that the sergeant had simultaneously dialed that number, and both received busy signals. We were able to chuckle about that afterwards but not while the fracas was escalating.

Once I was freed from the tier, I went to the barred doors of the dining room and saw the houseman throwing plastic cups and plates at the black inmate, hitting him with almost every one. The houseman was also shielding himself with a metal insert. His opponent tried in vain to block the dishes while swinging a spatula. I ordered them to stop fighting but they refused. The couple of dozen other inmates huddled in a corner away from the fight, and I watched one older black inmate chowing down fried eggs as fast as he could. After backup officers arrived, we ended the brawl, handcuffed all the inmates and started escorting them back to their cells. Someone asked the older black inmate why he was eating so many eggs in such a hurry and he replied, "I knew breakfast was definitely over once that fight started, so I grabbed as much food as I could." That was another humorous story to recall later on.   When we entered the dining room, I immediately restrained and handcuffed the young black inmate. As another officer and I removed him from the room, a wound on his head began bleeding profusely. He told us the white inmate had cut him open with the metal spatula. When the black inmate asked me how bad his injury was, I told him, "I can't see; there's too much blood!" He groaned and started to faint, so I placed a towel on his head to stop the bleeding and took him to the prison Hospital for treatment. He was confined in the Hospital lockup area, and I returned to the DSU to write a substantial incident report.

Members of the Inner Perimeter Security (IPS) team, including their lieutenant, were on site to begin an investigation. I explained to him what I knew about the disturbance and how I responded, but the lieutenant snarled at me, "Why didn't you run in there as soon as the fight started?" A person does not need to be a trained Correction Officer to know the folly of running alone into a prison fight inside a confined space with so many inmates possibly involved. We wait for support from other officers to avoid unnecessary injuries. My immediate respond to the lieutenant was, "I was waiting for the inmates to run out of dishes!" I was not about to have a plate bounced off my head for anyone! That was the final chuckle we were able to enjoy the next day.

Casualties

I doubt that any correctional facility can boast of never experiencing physical and psychological casualties among Correction Officers and support staff. MCI Norfolk is no exception.

A couple of veteran officers once described to me the murders of Officer James Souza and Industries Instructor Alfred Baranowski in 1972, four years before my career began. They told me that a woman had smuggled two handguns into the prison and gave them to the inmate she was visiting. There was no metal detector in operation at that time. The convict then forced his way out of the visiting room, shot Officer Souza, and headed into the prison yard with his female friend. He approached and killed Baranowski, whom he passed on the way back to his home unit. When an armed team arrived to confront the murderer, he reportedly shot and wounded his girlfriend and then committed suicide.

The next tragedy they described occurred in 1975 when another inmate somehow obtained a firearm and took Officer "Bill" hostage while he was conducting an hourly inmate count one night. A second officer backed up "Bill" during his rounds, while a third remained by the telephone in the unit office.

The story continued that while the inmate held his hostage, the other two officers vacated the building to avoid becoming additional captives. At some point, the inmate shot Officer "Bill" in the head, leaving him alive but gravely injured. Officer "Russell," who had been elsewhere when the shooting occurred, reportedly ran into the unit and offered himself as a substitute hostage so that Officer "Bill" could be taken for medical treatment. The inmate made Officer "Russell" undress, then shot him several times, but "Russell" was able to escape, running for safety and assistance. I was then told that two officers engaged the shooter with their own weapons. They shot and wounded the inmate, who then retreated upstairs in the unit. The story climaxed when another inmate living inside that unit told officers that he could talk the assailant into surrendering. They allowed him to climb out of a window, where he was confronted by a State Police officer. After Correction Officers identified him, the inmate was allowed to proceed. He re-entered the unit, retrieved the firearm and convinced the injured convict to surrender.

Officers "Bill" and "Russell" survived but were physically and psychologically scarred. The shooter was transferred to MCI Walpole to continue his prison sentence.

Several years later, an inmate friend of the assailant was being taken from Walpole to the MCI Norfolk Hospital. As he passed through the Pedestrian Trap corridor, he spotted a captain who was very familiar with the attacks in 1975, watching him from the control room. He looked at the captain, pointed his middle finger at him and shouted that the gesture was for all Norfolk officers, courtesy of the shooter. The captain became enraged, confronted him inside the trap, where the inmate promptly punched and knocked him down. The captain was not badly hurt, the convict was subdued by other officers, and hastily returned to Walpole.

Sometimes, assaults by inmates against staff can be avoided, but end up becoming learning experiences. For the first few years of my career, handcuffs and other restraint equipment were not allowed to be carried by officers inside the institution, even in the segregation unit. If a supervisor ordered that an inmate be taken to the RB and locked up, two officers were expected to escort him there, unrestrained and under his own power. I participated in many lockups this way, and my fellow officers and I knew such a method was an accident waiting to happen. The incident that finally prompted management to allow yard officers to carry handcuffs cost one 3-11 officer a serious eye injury. He and his partner were escorting an inmate to the RB but had no handcuffs with which to restrain him. The inmate suddenly swung and hit one of the men in the face. His partner physically subdued the assailant, and the two officers had to grapple with the inmate while carrying him to the lockup.

For quite some time, Correction Officer advocates have been bringing to light the reality of psychological problems, Post Traumatic Stress Disorder (PTSD), and even suicide caused by the difficulties of the job. I've always agreed with the analysis that the three most significant obstacles Correction Officers have to face are, first; prison administrations. History is replete with unfair labor practice complaints, violations of collective bargaining agreements, unreasonable discipline, and mistreatment of staff.

The second problem was our fellow employees. The union battles brought out the worst in many people who adopted a "might-is-right" syndrome. Harassment, intimidation, physical and mental abuse were rampant during these times. Then, we had to deal with ranking officers who occasionally overstepped their bounds, officers who would report others for alleged violations in exchange for promotions or favorable treatment, and simply irrational, uncivil people.

The inmates, our natural adversaries, were the least of our worries. Our relationship with them was generally understood to be professional, not personal.

Over the twenty-plus years I was involved with corrections, I witnessed far too many sad circumstances. One night in 1976 I was teamed with another 4-12 officer who had been bemoaning his many personal problems for several days. He spoke with the prison's Catholic priest and seemed to have calmed down towards the end of the shift. The next night, he was absent from roll call, and word came down that he had committed suicide with his own firearm.

The institution locksmith was a very disagreeable officer. Even when he was being honored as Employee of the Month, he gruffly stormed out of the ceremony, wanting no part of it. Not long after he retired, I read his obituary in a local newspaper. The life expectancy of a Correction Officer was reported to be 57 years but too many succumbed to the stresses of the job and failed to survive that long.

A well-liked female officer riding a motor scooter to work one day was struck by an automobile and killed. A male officer friend gave a tearful eulogy for her co-workers in the prison auditorium.

One easy-going House Officer found himself under investigation by internal security after he was seen driving a new, expensive car and carrying large amounts of cash. As a group of us entered the Ad Building for the Day Shift, IPS officers surrounded him, ordered him to stand and be pat searched. The subject stated something to the effect, "Oh, well, I guess you got me, it's in my underwear," and handed them a hidden cache of illegal drugs. By smuggling narcotics, he was endangering the safety of fellow officers and employees for the sake of earning some illicit cash.

The senior in charge of the RB on my first day was very friendly and commanded a lot of respect. He carried this persona into his promotion to supervisor and it seemed that his career was skyrocketing, but he left Norfolk under mysterious circumstances. No one seemed to know if he transferred, retired, resigned, or died, but rumor had it that he was wandering around the center green of a particular city, looking like a homeless person. By chance, I did see this former co-worker one day while I drove through that area, and he appeared as the rumors alleged.

During the collective rip-out by Walpole 10-Block inmates on the Second Floor RB, extraction teams restrained and transferred each one to a security cell, with every exercise being videotaped for the safety of all involved. In the aftermath, some of the inmates filed lawsuits against the Department of Correction and the extraction officers. The insanity of the liberal Massachusetts criminal justice system allowed these complaints to be heard in court. One of the officers recounted to many of us how attorneys for the inmates grilled him over and over in depositions, watching every frame of the videotapes, trying to find fault, and demanding that the officer explain each of his moves. Though the inmates lost their frivolous lawsuits, they still wasted enormous amounts of money, time and energy while inflicting undue stress upon several officers.

In 1989, I suffered a ruptured lumbar disk from an accident at home and was on medical leave for 30 days. During that time, an Hispanic inmate filed a lawsuit against the DOC and *me*, alleging that I stole his property. Prior to my injury, I had dealt with him on the third floor RB, inventoried and packed his property without incident after he had been transferred. During my recovery period, I received a phone call from a female DOC attorney who explained the details of this suit and asked me to travel to Boston for a deposition. I told her I was confined at home and couldn't drive or walk. I gave her my truthful version of

events and insisted that the complaint was totally frivolous. A couple of weeks later, the lawyer called again to tell me that the department had settled with the inmate! *Settled?* The lawsuit had **no** merit! She stated that the inmate had disappeared, his own attorney had no idea where he was, yet the department **still** paid out some kind of settlement! Light years beyond insane!

Another incident occurred during a Sunday in the RB. The 7-3 shift commander made an unscheduled security check of the building and when he reached the third floor, he discovered the sergeant sitting back at the office desk, reading a magazine; two officers watching a football game on an inmate's television set up on the tier; and a third officer asleep under a blanket on a table inside the medical examination room. A fourth officer was out of the building, escorting an inmate to the prison Hospital. Even though the tier was quiet and secure, the DOC frowned on officers being distracted from their areas of observation. The commander wrote reports against all the officers and they received various degrees of disciplinary action; even the officer who wasn't present at the time! Try to figure **that** out! Years later that uninvolved officer recalled the incident one day and made some observations. He told a group of us that the sergeant, who was initially disciplined, had shortly afterwards been promoted to lieutenant; of the two officers watching TV, one eventually rose through the ranks to become a captain, and the other was appointed by the superintendent to the IPS team; the officer who was sleeping was promoted to sergeant and given a job handling inmate property. The officer who wasn't even there but was still disciplined said disgustingly, "And I got holes in my pants and can't even get a new pair!" This was the DOC's version of fairness.

I noted earlier that former Disciplinary Lieutenant "Gib" was a very strange fellow. He had the demeanor of someone who, when the boss said "Jump," would ask, "How high?" He was so immersed in his job that he even failed to use his vacation weeks one year. At some point he was ordered to utilize that time off, and then he suddenly vanished from our ranks. The last rumor being passed around was that he was being investigated for a crime and had later committed suicide.

One incredibly bizarre event was completely harmless, but DOC management turned it into a criminal conspiracy. A black officer applied for a position on the Special Response Team and was interviewed by three white team members. All the participants were friends who worked together, socialized, and teased each

other without animosity. When he entered the interview room, two of the veteran team members were wearing white hoods as a joke. Everyone present had a good laugh, the black officer was accepted to the team, and nothing more was said. At some point afterwards, the black officer was sharing the comical story with others when he was overheard by an IPS officer. Apparently this eavesdropper couldn't simply ignore what he was hearing. Even though no one had been harmed, he felt he had to report it. The next thing they knew, the three interviewers were facing disciplinary hearings. The chairman of the panel was also one of the officers who had been caught watching TV in the third floor RB. Neither of these incidents hampered his later promotions. The two who were wearing the hoods were suspended without pay and removed from the SRT.

I represented them for the MCOFU at a DOC "kangaroo court" hearing and assured them afterwards that the union would support any appeals they desired. Surprisingly, both declined to contest their sanctions; one resigned and the other ultimately retired. Thanks to a single confused IPS officer, who apparently felt that he would have been in trouble if anyone found out that he had simply **heard** the story, two officers were punished and stigmatized for nothing!

Over my twenty years at Norfolk, I worked at different times with father and son officers. One such pair were friendly, likeable and respected; the father served mostly on the Midnight Shift, while the son worked the 7-3 shift. After I retired and was working as a Field Representative for the union, I was told that the son had been arrested by Massachusetts State Police for attempting to smuggle illegal drugs into the prison. There was nothing I or the union could do for him, since it was a criminal matter, but I never would have suspected him of committing such a violation. I could only imagine the pain his father was enduring over this situation, as his son was ultimately convicted and sentenced to prison time.

In the mid 1980s I helped break in a young man who became one of the best officers I ever worked with. He was competent in all phases of the job and eventually was promoted through the ranks to captain. One of the most nagging problems facing captains was that there hadn't been a Civil Service test for that position in quite some time, so prison superintendents were allowed to appoint them from the rank and file. Instead of maintaining Civil Service job security, they were beholden to their bosses and were sometimes pressured to perform tasks against their judgments or risk being demoted. This new shift commander exhibited some of that pressure after a time, and then sadly died of an apparent heart attack while exercising at home. He was not yet 50 years old.

As for me, I escaped my time of service with most of my "marbles" and body parts intact. I was physically assaulted by inmates four times but was never injured, thanks to timely assistance from fellow officers and my own self-defense skills. I was shoved, kicked, had water and projectiles thrown at me, and I lost count of the number of threats inmates made against me. Confrontations with convicts were an accepted aspect of this profession. Unreasonable treatment by management and personal conflicts with fellow staff members, however, were totally unacceptable and added to the difficulties of the job.

That's why it's said in so many circles that "we walk the toughest beat!"

IN MEMORY OF

CORRECTION OFFICER   INSTRUCTOR

JAMES R. SOUZA   ALFRED J. BARANOWSKI

KILLED IN THE LINE OF DUTY

JULY 31, 1972

A Cast Of Characters

For the most part, the officers and non-security personnel I worked with during my career at Norfolk were quality professionals who performed their duties to the best of their abilities. I never witnessed an officer failing to go to the aid of another, and teamwork was a common virtue. Still, as in most every line of work, there were plenty of real "characters" within the ranks, some of whom surprised co-workers by surviving till retirement.

The first one I encountered came in 1980; an officer named "Will" who was regularly late for his 12-8 shift. Management was obviously upset with his lack of responsibility and reassigned him to the 4-12 shift, perhaps figuring that the stern leadership of ADS "Arnold" would straighten him out. While waiting in the Gatehouse lobby to begin my 10-6 shift one night, I watched "Will" come strolling in around 9:30pm, uniform in hand, wearing fancy dress clothes. He changed into the uniform and reported for duty. "Arnold" was angrily staring at him through the control room windows, realizing that he was almost six hours late. A number of days later, "Will" was no-call, no-show again, but this time someone from the New York State Police reported that he had been killed in an automobile accident.

While working the 10-6 shift another night, my two partners and I met up with the 12-8 yard lieutenant while walking from one building to another during an hourly count of the One Block units. He glanced at Three Tower, pointed and queried, "What's that?" We could see flashing lights coming from inside the tower where it should have been dark. The lieutenant then exclaimed, "Either that guy is arc welding or he's watching TV!" He then went to inspect the tower and discovered that the officer had indeed smuggled a television into his post; a definite breach of regulations. The employee was ultimately terminated.

Fellow 4-12 Officer "John" was likely the strangest person many of us had ever seen. He was fanatically religious, a loud talker, and outlandishly opinionated. His most notable quirk was sifting through outside trash barrels to collect empty soft drink cans which he would redeem for cash. Shift commanders were apparently so skeptical of Officer "John's" abilities and his demeanor that they regularly assigned him to tower duty to keep him isolated. When he began

working on the Day Shift, Officer "John" was rotated through various posts, but after he was seen digging into trash cans inside the prison, he was relegated to tower duty once again. A few years later, I attended a retirement party for Officer "John" and a few other employees and while most folks were formally dressed, he was wearing full American Indian garb. I doubt that anyone ever tried to figure out this guy.

One of my best friends, Officer "J," was a laid-back officer who had experience on every shift. He did seem a little confused at times, though. One of the Day Shift commanders mentioned in conversation that he wanted the flexibility to rotate tower assignments, but a few officers, including Officer "J," were being regularly posted there. I suggested to the commander that he include Officer "J" in my regular RB crew. He would work well with us and the captain would have an open tower to use for assignment options. Officer "J" enjoyed working with the RB officers but he was prone to making mistakes, some serious.

Once, the RB sergeant sent him to escort an inmate into a general population housing unit and told him to return immediately. More than an hour passed and Officer "J" hadn't come back, so the sergeant began calling different areas of the prison trying to find him. Another officer happened to look out a window and see Officer "J" wandering around the Quad, chatting with different people, and called to him to return to the RB.

In a second incident, Officer "J" was assigned to the second floor RB control post. This area was to remain occupied, locked, and secure at all times. One of his fellow officers who was working on the tier told a few of us that he heard the telephone ringing for an unusually long time, walked to the control post, and found it empty. Officer "J" was nowhere to be found. The tier officer managed to reach the phone by poking a broomstick through the bars and said it was Officer "J" asking if anyone wanted lunch. He had locked the post, taken the keys and gone to the employee dining hall; definitely a breach of security and violation of policy and common sense. Fortunately, luck was with everyone involved and order was quickly restored.

Remembering the old saying that "there are no secrets in the big house," there was another disturbing story about Officer "J." I did not witness the incident, but it was reported that an inmate attempted to escape by hiding inside a 55-gallon drum of trash being trucked out of the institution from the Industries Building. Officer "J," on duty at the loading platform, was responsible for

checking every container for potential escapees. The inmate was apprehended by officers in the Vehicle Trap before he could flee the prison. I never heard if there was ever any disposition in this case.

The behavior of Officer "B" was difficult to fathom. He spent most of his career on the Midnight Shift, and he had the appearance of a lost soul. He boasted a resume' which included being a military veteran, a ballroom dancer, and a hairstylist, but Officer "B" was most famous for pleading with co-workers for advice on how to "get girls." He made newspaper headlines for posting signs in his yard that read, "I need a wife," and went missing for a period of time, which prompted police and neighbors to search for him. He even went so far as to take his story to Hollywood, where he allegedly used sick leave to appear on a television talk show with his "wife" signs in hand.

Officer "B" was a very mild-mannered man who endured more than his share of ribbing from other officers but could erupt in anger without warning. I believe he retired after completing twenty years of service and then faded into obscurity.

The most fascinating union grievance I generated and drove through the appeal process involved the refusal of the "Pete" administration to provide me with unredacted copies of incident reports written by two officers against another. Male Officer "Tim" and female Officer "Donna" had exchanged harsh words one morning while "Tim" was working in the First Floor RB control post and "Donna" was passing through his area. They didn't encounter each other for the remainder of the shift, but "Donna" and another male officer who overheard the conversation chose to write incident reports, alleging "Tim" threatened her. The superintendent made the correct decision to have the Personnel Director speak to the aggrieved parties separately in a role of "sexual harassment officer." He interviewed each person, essentially told both of them to "knock it off," and diffused a potential problem very informally.

There were no repercussions from this incident, but "Tim" and I, as his union representative, asked for copies of all the reports written against him. Our request was lawful and proper, but Supt. "Pete" would only allow us to have reports with individual names redacted. He claimed to be worried about retaliation, even after we assured him that the argument was settled peacefully. We viewed his lack of cooperation as defacto support for "Donna" and contempt for "Tim" and the union. I then initiated an appeal. At every level of the process, the union won the case and the superintendent was ordered by the appellate

authorities to provide unredacted reports. Supt. "Pete" defied the orders. When the appeal reached the Labor Relations Commission, that body also sided with the grievant, but Supt. "Pete" remained in defiance. Our final step was to take the case to Suffolk Superior Court for enforcement of the order. However, the MCOFU underwent a disastrous Executive Board election in March 1998. Four experienced members; the president, vice president, treasurer and grievance coordinator; were replaced by four inexperienced, ineffective Correction Officers, and the grievance that "Tim," the union and I had worked so hard to win was dropped by the new board and never found its way to court. The only record of this case that remains is in the historical archives of Massachusetts labor law. We never did receive the documents we requested.

Despite these infrequent foul-ups, the Correction Officers with whom I walked a beat at MCI Norfolk were an exemplary group of professionals. In my years behind the walls I viewed two inmate fatalities, only a few serious inmate injuries, and no remarkable officer assaults. A casual observer might expect more frequent physical confrontations to have happened during my time in the segregation unit, dealing with the most violent and problematic inmates, but training, teamwork and common sense among the officers prevented many potential security crises. We supported each other instinctively when called upon for assistance and responded quickly to inmate disturbances. Extractions from segregation cells were conducted according to DOC policy, as safely as possible for inmates and officers alike.

Outside of the inmate "strike" and mass transfers in 1978, I never experienced a situation where the security of the institution was in jeopardy. Stress and tension were always downsides of being law enforcement officers, as we had to be alert to prospective problems. Inmates had long hours to plan assaults and escape attempts, manufacture weapons, and disrupt the orderly running of the prison. In addition, correctional staff were often burdened by managerial mistreatment and personality conflicts among co-workers. Despite dealing with those aspects of the job, I enjoyed a successful career, made my contribution to humanity by protecting fellow citizens from convicted felons, and I'm proud to have served with such a capable and dedicated group of Correction Officers!

CORRECTION OFFICER'S PRAYER

Lord, when it's time to go inside that place of steel and stone

I pray that you will keep me safe so I won't walk alone.

Help me to do my duty, please watch me on my rounds

Amongst those perilous places, and slamming steel door sounds.

God, keep my fellow officers well and free from harm.

Let them know I'll be there, too, whenever there's alarm.

Above all when I walk my beat, no matter where I roam,

Let me go back from whence I came, to family and to home.

Epilogue

As I approached completion of my 20th year as a Correction Officer, my wife and I discussed an option: I could retire with a pension worth fifty percent of my salary at the time, or continue working for another disquieting ten years to earn a significant increase in pension. This was not a case of whether I could still **do** my Correction Officer job but whether I **wanted** to do it. One item that affected our decision was an offer by the MCOFU to become the union's second Field Representative.

I had long ago given up aspirations of furthering my career either through promotion or specialty service. Even though I was an experienced steward and staunch advocate for the union and its membership, the years of friction between employees who chose sides during the MCOFU-AFSCME war left noticeable scars on many personal relationships.

My wife and I were comfortable with our financial situation and agreed that the combination of my pension and her hairstyling business would suit our family needs. Any additional income would be profit. So, I completed the paperwork, retired from the DOC on August 2, and was hired as an MCOFU Field Representative on September 1, 1996.

I enjoyed serving my fellow union members and former co-workers in this new capacity, advocating for them at disciplinary hearings, grievance proceedings, and contract negotiations, assisting the Executive Board, plus editing the organization's weekly information bulletin and monthly newspaper. It was a pleasure being welcomed into a family of union E-Board members, office staff and employees. However, once again, a good thing came to an early end. The initial MCOFU Executive Board was comprised of seven volunteers; a president, vice president, treasurer, executive secretary, grievance coordinator, business agent and legislative representative. After the union was certified and the first collective bargaining agreement was secured, an official election was held to fill these positions. The originals remained in office.

In March 1998, though, some envious, disgruntled officers infected the membership with an anti-incumbent sentiment. Their false allegations and hateful rhetoric succeeded in replacing the experienced and accomplished union president, vice-president, treasurer and grievance coordinator with four untested, incompetent members. I was welcomed and encouraged by the new Board to stay on as Field Representative, but flatly refused. It would have been impossible for me to work productively with such a dysfunctional group. I resigned immediately, disposed of my files, and gave up a $600-a-week job, plus benefits, on **principle!** That was the end of my involvement with the Massachusetts Department of Correction.

Looking back one more time, I recall June 6, 1976 as being the 32nd anniversary of D-Day, the Normandy invasion in WWII. It was also my first official day as a Correction Officer at MCI Norfolk; and I returned for more!

On June 28, 1996, I completed my final 7-3 shift...in the RB, where I experienced my first inmate disturbance as a trainee! Where else? Coincidence?

I DON'T ALWAYS ENJOY
BEING A RETIRED
POLICE
CORRECTIONAL
OFFICER
...Oh Wait, YES I DO

Made in the USA
Middletown, DE
03 January 2020

82527105R00092